THE NATURE AND
CAUSES OF APOSTASY
FROM THE GOSPEL

THE TREASURES OF JOHN OWEN

———— ❋ ————

THE NATURE AND CAUSES OF APOSTASY FROM THE GOSPEL

Abridged and made easy to read by
R. J. K. Law

THE BANNER OF TRUTH TRUST

THE BANNER OF TRUTH TRUST
3 Murrayfield Road, Edinburgh EH 12 6EL
PO Box 621, Carlisle, Pennsylvania 17013, USA

*

© R J K Law 1992
First Published 1992
ISBN 0 85151 609 2

*

Typeset in 10½/12pt Linotron Baskerville
at The Spartan Press Ltd, Lymington, Hants
Printed and bound in Great Britain by
BPCC Hazell Books
Aylesbury, Bucks, England
Member of BPCC Ltd

Contents

1: *The Nature and Causes of Apostasy from the Gospel*

BACKGROUND HISTORY

The early church were careful whom they admitted into fellowship. Every Christian who sinned was only readmitted into fellowship by open repentance.

But where notorious and scandalous sins, such as murder, adultery or idolatry, were committed, no readmission into the fellowship of the church was allowed. This was especially so when a Christian committed idolatry through fear of being martyred for his faith.

The Church of Rome, however, was considered to be very remiss and lax in its discipline. Tertullian accuses Zephyrinus, Bishop of Rome, of admitting adulterers to repentance and readmission into the fellowship of the church.

Novatus and Novatianus opposed this laxity by going to the opposite extreme. They denied all hope of pardon and return to church membership to any person who sinned after baptism. But their followers, horrified at such extreme discipline, left all persons, upon their repentance, to God's mercy, refusing to readmit only those who had committed notorious and scandalous crimes.

This discipline they tried to establish from the nature of baptism, which was never to be repeated. They thought that no pardon could be granted to those who fell into sins from which they were cleansed at their baptism. This they supposed was taught in the Epistle to the Hebrews 6:4–6. So, as always happens when men think that they see some special teaching or doctrine in one text or passage of Scripture and will not bring their interpretation to the whole light of God's Word, these verses were sadly misunderstood and misused.

The Church of Rome, though judging rightly from other parts of Scripture, that the Novatians had transgressed the rule of charity and gospel discipline in their refusal to admit notorious sinners on their repentance back into church membership, yet did not know how to answer them from this text of Scripture. So, rather than open herself to adverse judgment and criticism, she withheld assent to the authority of this epistle. So it was just as well that some learned men, later on, by their sober interpretation of these words, plainly showed that this text did not support the errors of the Novatians. Without this, men would have upheld their own interpretations rather than submit to Scripture authority, which would have proved ruinous to the truth. But this epistle, given by God for the edification of the church, would in the end have prevailed, whatever interpretation men in their prejudices and ignorance put on its teaching.

But all this controversy is long since buried and churches today readmit into communion those who have sinned after baptism upon their repenting openly.

But the meaning of these words has been the subject of great debate at other times also.

Some suppose that this text describes true believers and so they teach that true believers can fall away and finally perish.

Others, teaching that believers in the covenant of grace cannot finally fall away and perish eternally, teach that true believers are not meant in these verses – or if they are, these words are only a warning and the means by which true believers are kept from falling away.

Some, on reading or hearing these words, think that because they have backslidden and neglected Christian duties after professing faith in the gospel, they must have committed those sins which are referred to in our text, and so are discouraged or believe that they are irretrievably lost.

But these verses discourage none from repenting of their sins and throwing themselves on God's mercy and finding acceptance with him. They do serve, however, as a warning to all careless believers.

HEBREWS 6:4–6

In studying the words in this text, we must see their context, the persons meant, and what is intended by these words.

The context. The text begins with the word 'For', which tells us to look back and find out the reason why these words were written. The words immediately preceding are: 'if God permits'. Later on, in v. 9, believers are described as those from whom the author was confident of better things, things which accompanied salvation, which suggests that the text does not refer to believers. Nevertheless, he gives them this warning so that they might not become such. He accuses them of being lazy and negligent. Instead of growing and increasing in the knowledge of their faith and in Christian practices, they were standing still, if not actually going back. So he warns them of their danger if they do not repent of their present behaviour. Not to grow in the knowledge of the gospel and in obedience to its duties is to be in danger of returning to that state of unbelief and ignorance from which they had been rescued, and of rejecting the gospel altogether. To warn them, he gives a description of the miserable state of those who seemingly began well, when they acknowledged openly their acceptance of the gospel, and then through idleness and negligence they slipped back into their old state and practices and so ended in apostasy. So we can see how useful severe warnings are in preaching the gospel.

[3]

The persons described. They were such as had, by the gospel, great spiritual privileges and advantages. These being despised and neglected, they found themselves in great danger of apostasy from which they could never recover (*Heb. 2:3*).

The privileges which these persons had lay in special works of the Holy Spirit. These works were special to the time of the gospel. They could not have been made partakers of them under the law in Judaism. So the Spirit in this sense was not received by 'the works of the law, but by the hearing of faith' (*Gal. 3:2*). These privileges testified that they had been delivered from the bondage of the law by a participation in that Spirit which was the great privilege of the gospel.

There is no clear mention of any covenant of grace or mercy on them or to them, nor of any duty of faith or obedience which they had done. They are not declared to be justified, sanctified or adopted as children of God. Later, when the writer of this epistle comes to declare his hope and persuasion that his readers were not of those he has described, nor were they such as would fall away into perdition, he does it on three grounds:

(1) True believers had characteristics which accompanied salvation. These things were inseparable from salvation. Therefore none of the things in this text are inseparable from salvation or else his argument that their state was safe would not hold.

(2) True believers are known by their obedience and by the fruits of faith in their lives. This was 'their work and labour of love towards the name of God' (*v. 10*). By this, our writer declares them to be different from those he has described, who were in danger of perishing eternally. But none can perish who have these fruits of saving faith and sincere love.

(3) True believers live under the care and faithfulness of God, who has promised to preserve them eternally. 'God is not unrighteous to forget.' But God has only promised to keep

[4]

from perishing eternally those who are in the covenant of grace. Yet no such thing is supposed concerning the persons described in the text. They are in no way described as those whom God has faithfully promised to keep safe for eternity, but rather the contrary. This whole description therefore refers to some gospel privileges of which those who claimed to accept the gospel were made partakers, whether they truly believed or not.

What those privileges are which do not accompany salvation we shall now see.

The first privilege is 'enlightenment'. They were 'once enlightened'. The Syriac translation has 'once baptized'. It is certain that in the early church, baptism was called 'illumination', and to 'enlighten' was used for 'baptize'. So the times of baptizing new converts were called 'days of light'. The Syriac interpreter must have had this in mind and the word 'once' suggests that there is something in this interpretation.

Baptism was to be celebrated only once according to the faith of the church in all ages. And they called baptism 'illumination' because being one ordinance of initiation, it brought the new convert into the privilege of sharing in the mysteries of the church. By baptism, therefore, converts were taken out of the kingdom of darkness into the kingdom of light and grace. This seems to add support to the view that baptism is meant in our text because baptism was also really the beginning and foundation of sharing in all the other spiritual privileges mentioned. It was usual in those days that when persons were baptized, the Holy Spirit came upon them and endowed them with extraordinary spiritual gifts which belonged especially to the days of the apostles.

This interpretation has so much to support it that I would be tempted to embrace it if the word 'enlightened' did not require another interpretation. It was a good while after the writing of this epistle and all other parts of the New

Testament, at least an age or two, if not more, before this word was used mystically to mean baptism. But in the whole of Scripture it has another meaning, denoting an inward work of the Spirit and not the outward administration of an ordinance. To take a word in a special way, different from its use in all other parts of Scripture – unless the text forces us to do so, which this text does not – is presumptuous. And as for the word 'once', it does not only refer to 'enlightened', but equally to all the other privileges given in this text. 'Once' signifies no more than that those described were really and truly partakers of these privileges and blessings.

To be 'enlightened' is to be instructed in the gospel. The Hebrew word 'to teach' is often translated by the Greeks as 'enlightened' (verses such as *Exod. 4:12*; *Psa. 119:33*; *Prov. 4:4*; *Isa. 27:11*). To 'teach' in Hebrew is translated in the Septuagint (the Greek Old Testament) as 'enlightened' (*Judges 13:8*; *2 Kings 12:2*; *17:27*). Paul uses the same Greek word for it in 1 Cor. 4:5: 'Who will bring to light the hidden things of darkness'; in 2 Tim. 1:10: 'Who . . . has brought life and immortality to light by the gospel'; also in John 1:9: 'That was the true Light which gives light to every man who comes into the world'. Christ 'gives light' by teaching.

Paul says, 'For it is the God who commanded light to shine out of darkness, who has shone into our hearts to give the light of the knowledge of the glory of God in the face of Jesus Christ' (*2 Cor. 4:6*). 'The light of the knowledge' means to be instructed in the doctrine of the gospel so as to have a spiritual grasp of it. And there are two things the gospel requires us to understand and grasp spiritually.

The gospel requires us to understand and grasp spiritually the things it brings to us by its light, or in other words, by the knowledge it gives us. It brings us 'life and immortality' (*2 Tim. 1:10*). By the gospel we are called 'out of darkness into his marvellous light' (*1 Pet. 2:9*). The world, without the gospel, is the kingdom of Satan (*1 John 5:19*). The whole of the world and all that belongs to the world lies under the power of the wicked one, the prince of the power of darkness, and so is full of darkness. The world is a 'dark place' (*2 Pet. 1:19*). In the world, ignorance, foolishness, errors and superstition dwell and reign. By the dynamic power of this darkness, men are kept from God and do not know where they are going. This is called 'walking in darkness' (*1 John 1:6*). And the opposite of 'walking in darkness' is 'walking in the light' (*1 John 1:7*). So this simply means walking in the knowledge of God in Christ by the gospel. So because of this instruction in the knowledge of the gospel, it is called 'illumination', since it is, in itself, light.

Now in order to understand and grasp these spiritual truths of the gospel, the mind itself needs to be 'illuminated'. The knowledge of the gospel expels that darkness, ignorance and confusion with which the natural mind is filled. The knowledge of the doctrines of the gospel concerning the person of Christ, of God's being in Christ reconciling the world to himself, of Christ's offices, work and mediation along with the other chief doctrines of divine revelation, sets up a spiritual light in the minds of men, enabling them to grasp and understand what before was utterly hidden from them whilst alienated from the life of God through their ignorance (*Eph. 4:18*). Of this light and knowledge there are several degrees, depending on how they are taught, the capacity they have to receive what is taught, and the effort they put into learning and remembering what they have been taught. But only by the doctrines of the gospel can the mind be illuminated and freed from darkness and ignorance (*2 Pet. 1:19–21*).

This is the first privilege which the people in our text had. They are those who were illuminated by the instruction they had received in the doctrines of the gospel and the impression made by this instruction on their minds by the Holy Spirit. This is a work common to believers and unbelievers alike.

So we learn three great truths:

It is a great mercy, a great privilege to be enlightened with the doctrine of the gospel and to have its truths impressed on our minds by the inward work of the Holy Spirit.

This great mercy and privilege may be lost by the sin of neglect, which will serve only to increase the sinfulness and condemnation of those who were once made partakers of this privilege.

Where there is a total neglect of this great privilege, with no attempt to grow in the knowledge of the gospel, the condition of such persons is very dangerous and could lead to final apostasy, from which they will find it impossible to repent.

So that we might examine ourselves to see if we are one of those who are described in this text, we need to find out what these privileges are which do not accompany salvation.

(1) *The first privilege is 'spiritual illumination'*

There is a knowledge of spiritual things that is purely natural and disciplinary and which can be arrived at without any special help or work of the Holy Spirit. With effort and study, a knowledge of the Scripture can be had as it can be with any other art or science.

The 'illumination' here meant, being a gift of the Holy Spirit, differs from and is exalted above natural knowledge because this illumination brings the one so illuminated nearer to spiritual things in their nature than ever natural knowledge could. Natural light finds the things of the Spirit foolish (*1 Cor. 2:14*). But spiritual illumination gives the mind some satisfaction, delight and joy in the spiritual blessings it reveals. Although the gospel may not be fully understood, yet this illumination reveals it as a 'way of righteousness' (*2 Pet. 2:21*). This excites the mind to take the gospel seriously.

[8]

Natural knowledge has little or no power on the soul, either to keep it from sin or to enable it to obey. Under this natural knowledge, many sinners rest secure and believe they will never perish. But spiritual illumination works effectively on the conscience and the soul, enabling it to abstain from sin and to carry out all known duties. So persons under the power of this illumination and its convictions often walk blamelessly and uprightly in the world and so do not bring Christianity into contempt with the world. This spiritual illumination is also accompanied with some spiritual gifts (*Matt. 7:22*). But natural light and knowledge stand alone and are not accompanied with spiritual gifts.

Spiritual illumination is not that light and knowledge which brings the soul to salvation and to a life of holiness, but it is the first step leading to it. Spiritual illumination may give the mind glimpses of the beauty, glory and excellence of spiritual things, yet it does not give that direct, steady insight which cannot be arrived at by reason, but which is only to be had by grace (*2 Cor. 3:18*; *4:6*). Neither does this spiritual illumination change or transform the soul into the image of Christ by imparting his nature into the will and heart as does saving light and knowledge (*2 Cor. 3:18*; *Rom. 6:17*; *12.2*).

(2) *The second spiritual privilege mentioned is that they have 'tasted the heavenly gift'*

We therefore ask what this heavenly gift refers to and what 'tasting' this gift means.

The 'gift of God' sometimes means the act of giving. 'Thanks be to God for his indescribable gift' (*2 Cor. 9:15*). This gift was God's granting to the Corinthians a free, charitable, generous spirit in ministering to the poor saints. This is called 'God's gift': 'According to the measure of Christ's gift' (*Eph. 4:7*) – that is, 'according as God is pleased to give and grant the fruits of the Spirit to men' (*Rom. 5:15–17*; *Eph. 3:7*).

[9]

Sometimes the gift of God means the thing given (*James 1:17*). 'If you knew the gift of God' (*John 4:10*), that is, the thing given by God, or to be given by God. Some think that Christ is meant by this gift, but the context makes it plain that it refers to the Holy Spirit, for he is that 'living water' which the Lord Jesus promised to give.

And so far as I can see, the 'gift', meaning 'what God gives', is everywhere used to refer to the Holy Spirit. If this is so, the 'gift' of Acts 2:38 ('You shall receive the gift of the Holy Spirit') does not mean that which the Holy Spirit gives, but means the Holy Spirit himself. The Holy Spirit is given in the power of his miraculous works (*Acts 10:45; 11:17*). The Holy Spirit, therefore, is the great gift of God under the New Testament.

The Holy Spirit is said to be 'heavenly' because he is from heaven. This may refer only to his work and power because they are heavenly as opposed to earthly and carnal. But chiefly it refers to his being sent by Christ after Christ had ascended into heaven and had been exalted to the right hand of God (*Acts 2:33*).

The promise of the Holy Spirit was that he should be sent from heaven or 'from above', as God is said to be 'above', which means the same as 'heaven' (*Deut. 4:39; 2 Chron. 6:23; Job 31: 28; Isa. 32:15; 24:18*). When the Holy Spirit came upon the Lord Christ to anoint him for his work, 'the heavens were opened' and he came from above (*Matt. 3:16*). At Pentecost, the Holy Spirit came on the apostles as 'a sound from heaven'. So he is said to be 'sent from heaven' (*1 Pet. 1:12*). So, though the Holy Spirit can for other reasons be said to be 'heavenly', which reasons are not to be absolutely excluded from the meaning of the term 'heavenly gift', yet his being sent from heaven by Christ after his ascension into heaven and his exaltation in heaven is what is chiefly meant by 'heavenly gift'.

The Holy Spirit, therefore, is this 'heavenly gift' mentioned in this text.

That which militates against this interpretation is that the Holy Spirit is clearly mentioned next. So why should he be mentioned twice?

In answer to this, I would say that it is natural to mention the same thing twice in different words for emphasis. And this is especially necessary when there are different aspects of the same thing, as there are here.

The privilege, 'having become partakers of the Holy Spirit', may be explanatory of 'heavenly gift'. This is usual in Scripture, so there is no reason to deny an interpretation so suited to this place and which the constant use of the word confirms because the same thing seems to be mentioned twice.

But the Holy Spirit is here mentioned as the great gift of gospel times, as coming down from heaven, not so that he is no longer in heaven, but because he has a special work to do on earth. And this work of the Holy Spirit was to change the whole institution of religious worship in the church of God. So in the next privilege, he is spoken of with respect to his outward works. But he was the promised heavenly gift to be given under the New Testament, by whom God would institute and ordain a new way with new rites of worship. To the Holy Spirit was committed the reformation of the church, whose time had now come (*Heb. 9:10*). The Lord Christ, when he ascended into heaven, left Old Testament worship as it had been since the days of Moses, even though he had made it virtually redundant. And he commanded his disciples not to attempt any alteration until the Holy Spirit was sent from heaven (*Acts 1:4, 5*). So when he comes as the great gift of God, promised for New Testament times, he removes all the old Mosaic worship. He does this by fully revealing that all that the Mosaic worship signified and

[11]

pointed to had now come. Now the Holy Spirit sets up the new holy worship of the gospel, which was to take the place of the old temple worship.

The Spirit of God, therefore, as given specifically to introduce the new gospel state in truth and worship, is the 'heavenly gift' mentioned. So the Hebrews are warned not to 'turn away from him who speaks from heaven' (*Heb. 12:25*). He who speaks from heaven is Jesus Christ, speaking now in gospel times by the 'Holy Spirit sent down from heaven'.

We now come to the interpretation of what it is to '*taste this heavenly gift*'. The expression 'taste' is a metaphor meaning nothing more than testing or trying something out. It is to 'experience' something. This is what happens when we taste food. We taste it before deciding whether to eat it or not. Tasting, therefore, does not include swallowing and digesting. When we taste something we do not like, we spit it out and refuse to eat or drink it. On the cross, Christ tasted the sour wine, and when he had tasted it, he would not drink it (*Matt. 27:34*).

In some passages of Scripture, 'to taste' seems to include actual eating. David swore an oath saying, 'God do so to me . . . if I taste bread or anything else till the sun goes down' (*2 Sam. 3:35*). But the meaning here is, 'I will not even taste bread, much less eat it, till the sun goes down'. So under his oath, it was impossible for David to eat at that time. And when Jonathan said that he only tasted the honey (*1 Sam. 14:29*), he was excusing himself and making it seem that he had not actually eaten the honey and so gone against Saul's command.

But this term is unquestionably used to describe someone experiencing something. The virtuous wife 'tastes that her merchandise is good' (*Prov. 31:18*). In other words, she tested her merchandise and found it to be good. So these people in our text are those who have tasted the work of the Holy Spirit and found it to be good.

[12]

Taste is often used to mean 'to experience' something: 'O taste and see that the Lord is good' (*Psa. 34:8*). Peter along the same lines says, 'if indeed you have tasted that the Lord is gracious' (*1 Pet. 2:3*). So 'taste' simply means 'to experience' something for myself.

The spiritual privilege, therefore, which these Hebrews had was an experience of the Holy Spirit as the gift of God offered in the gospel. They had experienced him as the revealer of truth and the One who brings in the new, spiritual, gospel worship. The glory and excellence of this new state brought in by the Holy Spirit they had tasted and experienced, a privilege which many had not had. And by this tasting they had become convinced that it was far more excellent than that worship which they had been accustomed to in the past.

They had experienced the glory of the gospel brought to them by the Holy Spirit sent from heaven and had been greatly impressed by it. But now they were in danger of neglecting and despising this privilege. They were tempted to leave the finest wheat for their old acorns.

So from our understanding of this great spiritual privilege we learn four great truths:

We learn that all gifts of God under the New Testament are heavenly gifts (John 3:12; Eph. 1:3). So beware of neglecting and despising them (*Heb. 2:3*).

We learn that the Holy Spirit is the great gift of God under the New Testament, given to reveal the mysteries of the gospel and to bring in the institution and ordinances of spiritual worship.

We learn that there is a goodness and glory in this heavenly gift which may be 'tasted' or experienced in some measure by those who never receive them in their life and power for salvation. They taste the word in its truth but not in its life-giving power. They experience the worship of the church in its outward order, but see and experience nothing of its inward spiritual beauty. They experience the gifts of the church, but not its graces.

We learn that to reject the gospel both in its truth and worship, after experiencing something of its richness and glory, is a great slight on God and brings that person into great spiritual danger of suffering God's wrath for ever.

(3) *The third privilege was that they 'were made partakers of the Holy Spirit'*

This spiritual privilege is placed in the centre of all the spiritual privileges mentioned here in this text. Two gifts precede it and two follow it. All these privileges come from the Holy Spirit and so all depend on our being 'partakers of the Holy Spirit'.

Now we become a partaker of the Holy Spirit only when we receive him, and he may be received by us to come and dwell in us, or simply to do his work in us or on us.

In the first way, 'the world cannot receive him' (*John 14:17*). That is why the world is opposed to true believers. Therefore, those meant in this text were in no way partakers of the Holy Spirit in this sense. He had not come to dwell in them for their salvation. They had not so received him as to have him dwell in them for their salvation.

But they had received and experienced his gifts. In this sense, they had become partakers of the Holy Spirit. They had been privileged to share, along with true believers, something of his spiritual gifts (*1 Cor. 12:11*). So Peter told Simon the magician that he had no part in spiritual gifts. He was not a partaker of the Holy Spirit (*Acts 8:21*). So to be partakers of the Holy Spirit is for people to have a share in his gifts and to experience something of his workings upon them and by them.

But aren't all the privileges mentioned in this text the gifts and works of the Holy Spirit? If being a partaker of the Holy

Spirit means being partakers of his gifts and workings, why is this privilege mentioned here in particular?

In answer to this, I would remind you that we have already seen how Scripture says the same thing in various ways in order to impress its statements on our minds. But here, the writer of this epistle would have these apostates know what a dreadful slight and insult they are putting on the Holy Spirit who has so graciously made them partakers of these great spiritual gifts.

This privilege of being partakers of the Holy Spirit may well have been put in the centre of the list to show how all these privileges depend on him. They were partakers of the Holy Spirit because it was he who had 'enlightened them', who was 'the heavenly gift' etc. In all these things, they had been made 'partakers of the Holy Spirit'.

This privilege showed that the Spirit had actually brought them into an experience of these things, not only because they had heard these things preached and saw them worked out in the church, but also because they themselves had been brought by the Spirit personally to experience these things themselves and so to be personally involved. It is one thing for a man to have a share in gifts and to benefit by the ministry of the gifts of the church, and quite another to be personally endowed with them.

To remind them, therefore, of the great privilege they enjoyed under the gospel, a privilege far above anything they had enjoyed under Judaism, for then they had not so much as heard whether there was a Holy Spirit (*Acts 19:2*); now they had been made personal partakers of him. What greater insult, then, could they offer the Holy Spirit than to neglect and despise this so great privilege? How much this would add to the wickedness of their apostasy!

From this we see that the Holy Spirit is with many only by his gifts and power, but he has not come to live in them and so they are not truly Christ's people (*Rom. 8:9*). Many are made partakers of him in his spiritual gifts who are never made partakers of him in his saving graces (*Matt. 7:22, 23*).

(4) *The fourth privilege these apostates had been given was the privilege of 'tasting the good word of God'*

The Greek word here used for 'word' means a word spoken. It is used in another sense, in this epistle alone, to mean the active power of God (*Heb. 1:3; 11:3*). But the chief use of this word in Scripture means 'word spoken'. When it is applied to God, it means his word as preached and declared (*Rom. 10:17; John 6:68*). So what these apostates had tasted was the gospel as preached.

But did they not enjoy the Word of God in their state of Judaism? Yes, they did, because to them 'were committed the oracles of God' (*Rom. 3:2*). But it is the Word of God as preached in the times of the gospel which is meant and concerning which such excellent things are spoken (*Rom. 1:16; Acts 20:32; James 1:21*).

This Word is said to be 'good', more desirable than honey or the honeycomb (*Psa. 19:10*). The promise of God in particular is called his 'good word' (*Jer. 29:10*). This is the 'good thing' that was promised (*Jer. 33:14*). And the gospel, which is the declaration of the fulfilment of God's promise to redeem his people from their sins by Jesus Christ, is the 'good tidings' of peace and salvation by Jesus Christ (*Isa. 52:7*).

They are said to 'taste' the Word just as they 'tasted' the heavenly gift. The writer of this epistle keeps to this word on purpose to show that these apostates were not of those who really receive, feed and live on Jesus Christ as he is offered to them in the gospel (*John 6:35, 49–51, 54–56*). It is as if he had said, 'I do not speak of those who have received and digested the spiritual food of their souls, and so have turned it into spiritual nourishment, but I speak of those who have so tasted the Word of God that they ought to have desired it as sincere milk for their spiritual growth and health. But instead they have neglected that good Word and have now turned away from it like children who despise the food set before them.'

We learn, then, that there is a goodness and glory in the Word of God which is able to attract and affect the minds of men who yet never come to sincerely submit to it in obedience.

We learn also that there is a special goodness in the Word of the promise concerning Jesus Christ and the preaching of its fulfilment.

The goodness and glory of the Word of God lies in its spiritual, heavenly truth. All truth is desirable and beautiful. When the mind of man receives the truth, that truth brings his mind to perfection, conforming it into its own image.

Whatever is true is also good. So truth and goodness are put together by Paul (*Phil. 4:8*). And as truth is good in itself, so its effect on the mind is good also. It gives the mind peace, satisfaction and contentment. Darkness, errors and falsehood are evils in themselves and fill the minds of men with pride, uncertainty, superstition, fear and bondage. It is the truth that sets the soul free (*John 8:32*). Now the Word of God is the only pure, unmixed and solid truth (*John 17:17*). Without the Word of God, the mind of man wanders about in endless conjectures. The truth of the Word of God alone is stable, firm and infallible. This gives rest to the soul. So, as it is infallible truth, giving light to the eyes and rest to the soul, it is the 'good word of God'.

The Word of God is good because of the good doctrines that are in it. The nature and properties of God are declared in this Word. God being the only good, the only source and cause of all goodness, and in whose enjoyment all rest and blessedness lies, the revelation made of him, his nature and attributes makes the Word of God good indeed (*John 17:3*).

[17]

If it is incomparably better to know God than to enjoy the whole world and all that is in it, that Word must be good by which he is revealed to us (*Jer. 9:23, 24*). The Word of God is exceedingly good also in the revelation of the glorious mystery of the Trinity. This is that mystery the knowledge of which is the only means to have a right understanding of all other sacred truths, and without it not one of them can be understood aright, nor can any of them bring us to that true goodness which God desires to see in us. This is that which alone will give true rest and peace to the soul. And the least true believer in the world, by faith and obedience, experiences the power of this truth even though he is not able to speak clearly of the Trinity to others. All grace and truth are built on the doctrine of the Trinity and from the Triune God they all derive their power to bring salvation to sinners. So it is a good Word where this mystery is revealed.

The Word of God is good also because in it is revealed the whole mystery of the incarnation of the Son of God, revealing the infinite wisdom, goodness and grace of God in sending him to be our Saviour.

It is the good Word of God because it reveals the mercy, grace, pardon, justification, adoption and all other wonderful blessings that become ours when we receive Christ and put our faith in him.

It is also the good Word of God because of its blessed effects (*Psa. 19:7–9*; *Acts 20:32*; *James 1:21*). There is nothing to compare with the excellence, worth and goodness which is in God's Word. So it is, indeed, the good Word of God.

Apostates taste this Word of God when they know it is true and when they acknowledge it as true. This gives some peace to their minds, though they remain unrenewed. They that heard John the Baptist preach the truth rejoiced in its light because they found much that satisfied them (*John 5:35*). It

[18]

was the same with others who heard Christ preach (*Luke 4:22; John 7:46*). When men, through the knowledge of our Lord and Saviour Jesus Christ, escape the pollutions that are in the world through lust and forsake the company of those that live in error, they taste a goodness and sweetness in God's Word which brings rest and satisfaction to their minds. They then suppose they have arrived at salvation itself, not realizing they have only as yet 'tasted the good word of God'.

As to the doctrines and teachings which are in the Word, they have a taste of their goodness because these teachings give them hope of a future enjoyment. Mercy, pardon, life, immortality and glory are proclaimed in 'the good word of God'. These truths they taste with much joy and satisfaction and think that because they have tasted them, they have truly received them and are living in submission to them. But not having really received them and not being deeply rooted in them, when the heat of persecution rises, they fall away (*Matt. 13:20*).

By this tasting, they may feel many effects of the Word on their minds and consciences and experience something of its power on them. This tasting may be accompanied with delight, pleasure and satisfaction when they hear the Word preached (*Ezek. 33:30–33*). They like to hear but they do not receive into their hearts what they hear. Herod heard John the Baptist gladly and did many things, but there was only tasting and no receiving of the Word. Crowds also pressed after Christ to hear the Word, but few actually received it. So it is also with many in our day.

This tasting not only gives delight in hearing but some joy also in the things heard. Such are the hearers of the Word whom our Saviour compared to stony ground. They receive it with joy (*Matt. 13:20*), as did the hearers of John the Baptist (*John 5:35*). The Word, as tasted only, has this effect on their minds, rousing them to joy in the things which they hear. But this joy is not solid, abiding joy. It is not that joy unspeakable and full of glory which belongs only to true believers (*1 Pet. 1:8*). Their joy is like the morning mist which soon disappears. They rejoice at the thought of mercy, pardon, grace, immortality and glory, but make no effort to make sure that they have received these things for their own salvation.

The tasting of God's Word may well bring about a change and reformation in their lives so that they are ready to carry out many duties (*2 Pet. 2:18, 20; Mark 6:20*).

The word of the gospel, and Christ preached in the gospel, are the food of our souls. True faith not only tastes it, but feeds upon it, turning it into grace and spiritual nourishment in the heart. To really feed on God's Word, then, we must first lay it up or treasure it in the heart (*Luke 1:66; 2:19*). No nourishment will ever be obtained by food unless it is received into the stomach, where it is digested and passed on to nourish the whole body. In the same way, if God's Word is not received into the heart by meditation and delight, it may please for a while, but it will not nourish the soul.

Food must be mixed with the digestive juices or it will not nourish. Give a man never so much food, but if he suffers from lack of digestive juices, then that food will not be able to be taken in by the body for its nourishment. So until the Word received in the heart is digested by faith, it will not nourish our souls (*Heb. 4:2*). How different all this is from mere tasting.

When men feed on the Word, it is turned into a principle of life, spiritual strength resulting in spiritual growth – something which tasting alone cannot do. As food, when it is digested, turns into flesh, bones and blood, so does Christ and his Word bring life to our souls. Christ becomes 'our life' and 'lives in us' as the dynamic cause of our spiritual growth (*Gal. 2:20; Col. 3:3*). We grow spiritually by the Word (*1 Pet.*

2:2). A mere taste, though it may bring momentary refreshment, yet it communicates no abiding strength. So many may enjoy the Word when it is preached, but never receiving it by faith into their hearts, they never come to spiritual life, strength or growth.

The Word truly received will transform the soul into the likeness of God, who sends us this food to change us and make us like him in 'righteousness and true holiness' (*Eph. 4:21–24*; *2 Cor. 3:18*). Mere tasting will do nothing of this, and nor will it give us such a love of the truth that we remain faithful to it in all trials and temptations (*2 Thess. 2:10*). Nor will tasting bring forth the fruits of obedience to the Word.

(5) *The last privilege mentioned is 'and the powers of the age to come'* These they had also tasted by personal experience. These powers of the world to come are the mighty, great, miraculous operations and works of the Holy Spirit. These signs, wonders and mighty works, wrought by the Holy Spirit, were foretold by the prophets (*Joel 2:28–32*; *Acts 2:16–21*). It is possible that these apostates were partakers of these powers, in the gift of tongues and other miraculous works. Therefore, to slight the Holy Spirit who had endowed them with such powers made their sin very great, amounting to blaspheming against him, which would make their recovery impossible. They were rejecting the truth which had been confirmed by God with signs and wonders and with various miracles and gifts of the Holy Spirit (*Heb. 2:4*). How, then, could they escape when they neglected and despised so great a salvation which had been confirmed by these supernatural gifts of the Holy Spirit? (*Heb. 2:3, 4*.)

Ordinary gifts of the Holy Spirit are also 'the powers of the world to come'. So is everything that belongs to the kingdom of Christ. When a kingdom is first set up, great and mighty power is needed. But when it has been set up, ordinary powers will preserve it. So it is with Christ's kingdom. The

[21]

extraordinary miraculous gifts of the Spirit were used in the setting up of Christ's kingdom, but that kingdom is continued by ordinary gifts. Therefore they also belong to 'the powers of the world to come'.

From all these spiritual privileges we can now clearly understand who are the people whom the writer of this epistle had in mind.

It is clear that they are not true and sincere believers. There is no mention of faith or believing. There is nothing which makes us think they had any special relation to God in Christ. They are not described as 'being called according to God's purpose'. They are not described as having been born again. They are not described as being justified, or sanctified, or united to Christ, or the sons of God by adoption.

On the other hand, they are described as ground on which the rain often falls, but which bears nothing but thorns and briers (*v. 7*). But this is not true of real believers, for faith itself is a herb especially grown in Christ's enclosed garden. The writer of this epistle, describing true believers, distinguishes them from apostates. In believers he is confident of finding better things, things that accompany salvation (*v. 9*). Believers are known by their 'work and labour of love', because it is true faith alone which works by love (*v. 10*). But not one of these things is said of the apostates.

Of believers, the writer of this epistle asserts their eternal preservation because of the righteousness and faithfulness of God, and because of the immutability of his counsel concerning them (*vv. 10, 17, 18*). In all these and in many other ways, believers are distinguished from apostates.

It is clear that the persons in this text are those who have had special spiritual privileges.

They had received extraordinary gifts of the Holy Spirit, such as speaking in tongues or working miracles.

[22]

They had found in themselves and others convincing evidences that the kingdom of God and the Messiah, which they called 'the world to come', had come to them, and they had experienced something of its glories and were satisfied. Such persons as these, with their minds enlightened and their hearts touched, were probably held in high esteem amongst believers.

So there must be some malicious enmity against the truth and holiness of Christ and the gospel, some violent love of sin and the world, that could turn such persons as these from the faith and blot out all that light and conviction of truth which they had received. So we learn that the least grace is a better security for heaven than the greatest gifts or privileges whatever.

'*If they fall away*'. It is supposed by the writer of this epistle that these apostates may well fall away. From the example of Peter who denied Christ and was yet renewed to repentance, we say that there is no particular sin that any man may fall into occasionally, through the power of temptation, that can bring the sinner into that state from which it would be impossible to renew him to repentance.

This 'falling away', therefore, must refer to continued persistent rebellion and disobedience to God and his Word. A man may so fall into sin as still to retain in his mind such a principle of light and conviction that brings him back to repentance and acceptance with God. To exclude such from all hopes of repentance goes against the whole tenor of Scripture truth (*Ezek. 18:21*; *Isa. 55:7*). So men, after some conviction and reformation of life, may fall into corrupt and wicked ways and continue long in those ways. One great example is the wicked king Manasseh, who in the end repented and was restored and accepted by God. So whilst there is in such persons any seed of light, or conviction of truth which is capable of being revived, so as to once again

[23]

work powerfully in the soul, they cannot be looked on as apostates whom it is impossible to restore to repentance, though they are most certainly living dangerously.

Paul makes a distinction between 'stumbling' and 'falling' (*Rom. 11:11*). Paul never said that the Jews had arrived at that state where they had absolutely and irrecoverably fallen away. The same word for 'stumble' is used here but with a preposition attached increasing the force of their stumbling, either in the dreadful and fearful way by which they came to stumble, or else to suggest that their stumbling resulted in a violent fall.

From what has been said, it is clear what is *not* meant by 'falling away':

(1) It is not a falling into this or that actual sin of whatever nature that sin may be.

(2) It is not a falling into some temptation, for we have plenty of scriptural examples of those falling into various temptations and then being restored to repentance. This falling into temptation is not premeditated and does not come about by deliberate choice.

(3) It is not a falling which involves renouncing some important and essential principle of the Christian religion. The Corinthians fell in denying the resurrection of the dead, and the Galatians by denying justification by faith in Christ alone.

This falling away, then, must lie in a *total renunciation* of all the chief principles and doctrines of Christianity. Such was the sin of those who renounced the gospel to return to Judaism. This is the falling away referred to in this passage of Scripture.

For this falling away to be complete and final, this renunciation must be declared openly so that the person is seen to abandon Christianity completely for Judaism or for some other religion or to return to paganism. Some, in their hearts and minds, utterly renounce the gospel, but for fear of secular interests of one sort or another, keep up the appearance of still being believing Christians. Thus, they seek to cover their apostasy from the sight of men. But God is not mocked, and this utter dishonesty increases the gravity of their sin and brings upon them even greater judgments.

So we can define this 'falling away' as a voluntary, resolved renunciation of the faith, rule and obedience of the gospel, which cannot be done without bringing the highest reproach and contempt on the person of Christ himself.

WHAT THIS TEXT SAYS OF SUCH APOSTATES

It is impossible to renew them to repentance.

To be renewed to repentance is denied them; in fact it is *'impossible'* to renew them to repentance.

Some think that this is an absolute impossibility, whilst others think only a moral impossibility is meant. To decide the true meaning of this 'impossibility', the following principles need to be taken into account:

(1) *All future events depend on God, who alone necessarily exists*

Nothing exists or ever happens except by the will of God. So things that are future may be said to be *impossible* because God has decreed it should not exist or that event should not happen. So it was impossible that Saul and his posterity should be preserved in the kingdom of Israel. It was not contrary to the nature of God, but God had decreed that it should not be (*1 Sam. 15:28, 29*). But God's decree concerning the salvation of those whom he has chosen to save irrespective of their worthiness cannot be meant here in this text. God's decree concerning persons makes a difference between persons who are otherwise in the same state or condition (*Rom. 9:11, 12*). God's decrees are secret to himself, locked up in his mind, and therefore cannot be known by man until they have come to pass in the outworkings of history (*Isa. 40:13, 14*; *Rom. 11:34*).

(2) *Things are impossible because of what God is in himself*
It is impossible for God to lie. It is impossible that God should forgive sin without satisfaction being made to his justice and law because he will uphold the honour of his law. In this sense, the repentance of these apostates, *it may be*, is not impossible. I say *it may be*. It may be there is nothing contrary to the nature of God to bring apostates to repentance. But I will not be absolutely positive about this because the reason given for the impossibility of renewing them to repentance is that they 'crucify the Son of God afresh and put him to an open shame'. It may be that the righteousness, holiness and glory of God as the supreme ruler of the world makes it impossible to have any more mercy on them than on the devils themselves or those that are in hell. But I will not assert this to be the meaning of this passage.

(3) *Things are possible or impossible with respect to the rule and order of all things that God has appointed*
God has neither commanded us to try and renew these apostates to repentance. He has not given us the means of renewing them to repentance, nor has he promised to help us if we attempt to renew them to repentance. Therefore we should look on any attempt to renew these apostates to repentance as impossible. 'Without faith it is impossible to please God' (*Heb. 11:6*). Because God has not given us a command, or any means, or promised any help, we cannot attempt to renew apostates to repentance as an act of faith in God. So if we attempted to renew apostates to repentance, we would be doing it wilfully with no command or promise of help from God. So we would never succeed and nor would we ever please God by attempting it, for we would be doing something not motivated by faith, and any act not motivated by faith in God's revealed will and promise of help is sin (*Rom. 14:23*).

[26]

We are, therefore, to look on any attempt to bring apostates to repentance as impossible for us. For all we know, what is impossible for us is still possible for God. But our duty is to do only those works which God has prepared for us to walk in and attempting to renew apostates to repentance is not one of those works. What he will do is one thing. What he expects us to do, or not even attempt to do, is another.

That which is said to be impossible is 'to renew these apostates again to repentance'. The Greek word used in the New Testament for 'repentance' means 'a gracious change of mind', brought about by gospel principles and promises, leading the whole soul to conversion to God.

It is impossible 'to renew'. In the Greek, the words are 'again to renew to repentance'. Now does this mean: 'it is impossible for the apostates to renew themselves to repentance'; or is it: 'it is impossible for anyone to renew these apostates to repentance'? I judge that the latter is meant, because the impossibililty refers to the duty and efforts of others. For any to attempt to renew these apostates to repentance would be useless and a waste of time because it is impossible for them to be renewed to repentance.

Now the word 'renew' refers to the renovation of the image of God in our nature and our dedication again to him. We had lost the image of God by sin and were therefore separated from him. So this renewing concerns both the restoration of our nature and the dedication of our persons to God.

This renewal is either inward and real, or merely an outward confession of faith, sealed by an outward sign and pledge of this confession.

We are renewed inwardly by the regenerating and sanctifying work of the Holy Spirit (*Titus 3:5; I Thess. 5:23*). But this is not what is meant here, for these apostates had never been regenerated and sanctified, so could not be said to be renewed again to it.

In this passage, renewal can only refer to the outward confession of faith, sealed by an outward sign and pledge of that confession. Renovation in this sense concerns the profession of repentance towards God and faith in our Lord Jesus Christ, sealed by the outward ordinance of baptism. This was what was required from all who were converted to the gospel. But these apostates, though they made an outward profession of repentance and faith and had been baptized, had not been regenerated and sanctified. So it was from the outward renovation that these apostates fell away, totally renouncing the Christian faith and their baptism.

To renew them again, then, would be to bring them again to profess repentance towards God and faith towards our Lord Jesus Christ, and to receive again the outward sign and pledge of baptism. This is what is said to be impossible for anyone to bring about with these apostates.

So nowhere in this text is anything said concerning the acceptance and refusal of any who do truly repent. Nor does this text bar any who, having fallen by any great sin or who have returned to sinful ways and have long continued in those sinful ways and then, being convicted, desire to repent in all sincerity, from being accepted back into the fellowship of the church.

This text therefore greatly encourages such sinners and assures them that they are not the ones described in this text. But it also issues a warning to all who may be tempted to go back to Judaism or to their old state in which they lived before they were baptized into the Christian faith.

In the preaching of the gospel, then, it is necessary to make clear to men, and to insist on, the severity of God in dealing with apostate sinners.

We are not only to hold before men God's goodness, but his severity also (*Rom. 11:22*). So the writer of this Epistle to the Hebrews teaches us that God 'is a consuming fire' (*Heb.*

12:29). He would have us know that God is infinitely pure, holy and righteous and so may suddenly and unexpectedly treat us with the utmost severity if we neglect to seek for 'grace to serve him acceptably with reverence and godly fear'.

This severity of God in his dealing with rebellious apostates according to his holiness and wisdom is given to us as an example of how he may well deal with us if we provoke him in the same way. There are some sins, or degrees of sinning, that neither the holiness, nor majesty, nor wisdom of God can allow to pass unpunished, as an example to others who are tempted to go the same way. In such cases, God is said to exercise his severity.

God's severity is seen in outward judgments upon reckless, notorious sinners, especially the enemies of his church and glory (*Nahum 1:2*).

To make the world sit up and take note of his severity, God's judgments must be *unusual* (*Numb. 16:29, 30*). His judgments must also be evident and clear to all. 'He repays those who hate him to their face' (*Deut. 7:10*). When God says he will repay them to their face, he means he will do it openly and in the sight of all. So 'when they say, "Peace and safety!", then sudden destruction comes upon them' (*1 Thess. 5:3*). This is what will one day happen to the Romish Babylon and all who support her (*Rev. 18:7–10*). But these are not the judgments chiefly intended in this passage of Scripture.

God's severity is also seen in spiritual judgments, by which he leaves apostates under the sentence of never being able to be renewed to repentance. In this judgment there is a sentence of eternal damnation (*1 Tim. 5:24*). God so passes judgment on them in this world that they can never escape his eternal wrath in the next.

God takes no more interest in them and expects no spiritual fruit from them. When God graciously provides the means to conversion and repentance, he is described as looking for fruit, just as when a person plants a vineyard, he expects to get fruit from it (*Isa. 5:2, 4*). So when God no longer gives a person the means to repent, he no longer expects the fruits of repentance, and just as no-one looks after and cares for a desert, so God no longer looks after and cares for them as he does his own people.

God inflicts on them hardness of heart and blindness of mind so that they never will repent or believe (*John 12:39, 40*).

God may, in his severity, give them up to vile lusts (*Rom. 1:26, 28, 29*). In these lusts they are held as if by cords and chains, making it utterly impossible for them to rise up and repent.

God sends upon them a strong delusion that they should believe a lie, so that those who did not believe the truth might be damned (*2 Thess. 2:10–12*). The truth of the gospel was preached to them, and for some time was professed by them. They received the truth, but they did not love the truth so as to submit to it and obey it. So they were barren and unfruitful. But this was not all. They had pleasure in their sins, lusts and unrighteousness and were determined not to repent of them. These sins being condemned and judged by the gospel, they began to dislike and secretly hate the truth itself. But finding they needed to keep up appearances, they were ready to receive anything that was offered to them which did not require them to forsake these sins. In this state, God gives them up to the power of Satan, who blinds, deludes and deceives them with his lies which, under God's judgment, they readily believe and accept. And this is why so many who want to keep up the outward appearance of being Christian, yet do not want to forsake their sins and lusts, readily accept the Romish idolatry.

So what hope have apostate sinners, forsaken by God, of ever being renewed again to repentance?

There is a proneness in corrupted human nature to 'despise the riches of the goodness, forbearance and longsuffering of God, not knowing that the goodness of God leads them to repentance' (*Rom. 2:4, 5*). So in their spiritual hardness and their impenitent hearts, they treasure up for themselves wrath in the day of wrath and revelation of the righteous judgment of God.

So we see of what great importance it is to preach not only the goodness of God, but his severity also. We are to warn all men of the danger of apostasy, for in such a state no repentance will be granted to them.

We are to warn all who are in danger of such apostasies that 'if anyone so draw back, God's soul will have no pleasure in him'. We are to warn them that 'it is a fearful thing to fall into the hands of the living God'. We are to warn them that God will harden such sinners and 'give them up to strong delusions, that they may be damned'. We are to warn them that he has not promised to renew them to repentance, but rather has uttered many severe threats. They are like 'trees twice dead, plucked up by the roots', for which there is no hope. They have denied 'the Lord that bought them', and so they bring on themselves swift destruction.

It is true that this passage refers firstly to those who had, in the days of the apostles, received extraordinary or miraculous gifts of the Holy Spirit. But by a just analogy, this warning may be extended to others, now that those miraculous gifts have ceased in the church. Ordinary gifts and privileges which the Holy Spirit gives today equally oblige us to continue faithful to the gospel, and so this warning is still as relevant today as it was when first written. 'Let us not then be high-minded, but fear.' It is not safe to go too near the edge of a precipice.

The reason why it is impossible for apostates to be renewed to repentance

Some Greek manuscripts do not have the Greek word 'to themselves'. So the following interpretation of this phrase, though not that which is commonly received, is possible.

It is impossible that any should renew these apostates to repentance, for this cannot be done without crucifying the Son of God again. These apostates had utterly rejected Christ as crucified for them and had openly renounced all benefits they had received from his death. So to renew them to repentance would mean having to crucify Christ all over again, which cannot be done. 'If we sin wilfully after we have received the knowledge of the truth, there no longer remains a sacrifice for sins, but a certain fearful expectation of judgment, and fiery indignation which will devour the adversaries' (*Heb. 10:26, 27*). Christ cannot be offered again, and so crucified again. So their sins cannot be expiated. The unbloody sacrificing of Christ every day in the mass was not yet invented. But the writer to the Hebrews was referring to the Old Testament sacrifices for sin under the law. Because they could only legally expiate sins that had been done in the past, their offering needed to be frequently repeated for further sins committed. So from time to time when they sinned, a new sacrifice had to be offered for those sins. This could now no longer happen.

Christ being once offered for sin, whoever rejects that offering and does not believe that it expiates his sins has no other sacrifice to turn to. 'Christ dies no more.'

The *one* sacrifice of Christ deals with all sins, past, present and future, and those sins for which there were no sacrifices under the law. 'By him everyone who believes is justified from all things from which you could not be justified by the law of Moses' (*Acts 13:39*). There were some sins under the law for which no sacrifice was provided. He who was guilty of them was to die without mercy. Examples of such sins are murder and adultery. So David, having committed both these sins, says, 'For you do not desire sacrifice, or else I would give it' (*Psa. 51:16*). But Christ's sacrifice atoned for these sins also.

In the case of apostasy, there was no sacrifice either in the Old Testament or the New. Under the Old Testament there was no sacrifice appointed for one who had totally apostatized from the fundamental principles of the law or sinned 'presumptuously'. This was that 'despising of Moses' law', for which those that were guilty were to 'die without mercy' (*Heb. 10:28*). And so it is also under the gospel.

Wilful apostates, forfeiting all claim to the sacrifice of Christ, find no other sacrifice appointed for them. Instead, they find that God will cut them off and destroy them.

God has confined all hopes of mercy, grace and salvation to the one single offering and sacrifice of Jesus Christ (*Heb. 9:25–28; 10:12, 14*). Infinite wisdom and sovereign pleasure have put all grace, mercy and blessedness in Christ alone (*John 1:14, 16, 17; Acts 4:12; Col. 1:19*). And this 'one offering' of his is so sufficient and so powerfully effective to all that come to faith in Christ that no sinner who has come to this one sacrifice ever complains of there being only one sacrifice for sins and no more. If any reject and despise this one sacrifice, they have only themselves to blame. And they will not find any of those blessings which this one sacrifice of Christ brings by fleeing to other sacrifices which they have invented, such as the mass.

But the context makes this 'crucifying again' the work of the apostates themselves. 'They crucify him again to themselves.' They cannot physically crucify Christ again, but they do it morally. By their apostasy, they crucify again the Son of God to themselves.

They crucified Christ again by approving of and justifying that act of the Jews who had crucified Christ as an evildoer.

[33]

The Lord Christ must be accepted and received as the Son of God, and his gospel must be obeyed, or he must be seen as justly crucified as a deceiver, a blasphemer and an evildoer.

Jesus Christ claimed to be the Son of God and stood by that claim even to the death of the cross. Therefore he must either be accepted as the Son of God or rejected as an evildoer. These apostates rejected Christ as Son of God and declared him to be an evildoer, and so they renounced Christianity and went back to Judaism.

They also crucified Christ afresh by declaring that having tried him, his gospel and his ways, they found no truth or goodness in them. The motto of Julian the apostate was, 'I have read, known and condemned' your gospel.

Now no-one living can bring higher dishonour against Jesus Christ, in his person or in any of his ways, than openly to declare that having tried him and his gospel, they found nothing in them to be desired.

By these words they declare that if Christ came back to earth again in the flesh, they would crucify him again.

This sin was bad enough. But it was made worse because it was the 'Son of God' they crucified again to themselves.

The Jews crucified Christ when he was still in his state of humiliation, when he had 'emptied himself, and made himself of no reputation', so that it was not easy to look through the veils of his outward weakness and condition in this world, to 'see his glory, the glory of the only-begotten of the Father'.

But these apostates were crucifying afresh him who had been 'declared the Son of God with power, according to the Spirit of holiness, by the resurrection from the dead'. The greatness of this sin of apostasy was that it was directed against him who had been declared 'Son of God'.

Their sin was also made increasingly worse because by their apostasy they 'put him to an open shame'. They exposed the Son of God to public contempt. The Greek word used for 'open shame' means to bring any supposed offenders to such public punishment as is shameful in the eyes of men, so that all who see them look on them with loathing. The same word is used of Joseph when he discovered that Mary was with child (*Matt. 1:19*). He was 'not willing to make her a public example', that is, he did not wish to expose her to a shameful punishment as an example to others who might also be tempted to commit adultery.

So the writer of this epistle says of Christ, 'He endured the cross and despised the shame' (*Heb. 12:2*). On the cross he suffered dreadful pain, and was put to open shame. The death of the cross was especially shameful in those days. So the sin of these apostates does the same. They 'crucify him afresh, and they put him to open shame'.

'But if those who actually crucified the Son of God on earth and put him to open shame obtained mercy and pardon, why cannot these apostates also obtain mercy and pardon?'

I answer that the sin of those who forsake Christ and the gospel, after they are convinced of its truth, is far greater than the sin of those who crucified him physically.

The sin is greater because they were not ignorant of what they were doing. Those who crucified Christ in the flesh were ignorant of what they were doing (*Acts 3:17; 1 Cor. 2:8; 1 Tim. 1:13*).

These apostates had experienced the truth, goodness and glory of the gospel, which those who actually crucified him had not, nor could have. These apostates had 'tasted the good word of God, and the powers of the world to come'.

The actual crucifixion of Christ opened the way for mercy and grace to be communicated to men by the Spirit. But these apostates, having rejected even the work and grace of the Spirit, had no further door of mercy and grace opened to them.

There was in the sin of these apostates blasphemy against the Holy Spirit. They had experienced him and his powers by which he vindicated Christ and his gospel. Therefore they could not renounce the Lord Christ without ascribing these works of the Holy Spirit to the devil.

Paul says, 'No man speaking by the Spirit of God calls Jesus anathema' or 'accursed' (1 Cor. 12:3). To call Jesus anathema is to declare that he was justly crucified as an accursed person, as a public pest. This was what these apostates were doing. But this no-one can do who is filled with and led by the Holy Spirit. So as these apostates had the testimony of the Spirit to the truth and goodness of Christ and his gospel, they now, by their apostasy, crucified the Son of God afresh and put him to open shame, in spite of what they had learned by and from the Holy Spirit.

2: *Partial Apostasy from the Gospel*

It is in his gospel and church alone that Christ can now suffer at the hands of men. When any important principle of evangelical truth is forsaken and renounced; when gospel obedience is persistently neglected; when men begin to believe other things than what it teaches and do not live as the gospel requires, then we have a partial apostasy.

Men are apt to please themselves and to think well of themselves. Churches are happy if their outward ceremonies and orders of service are maintained, especially if it brings them secular advantages. The judgment of Christians about their churches is often quite different from the judgment of Christ.

The church of Laodicea was thought to be 'rich, wealthy and needing nothing'. But Christ declared that they were ignorant of the church's true state. In his eyes they were 'wretched, miserable, poor, blind and naked'. This was the judgment of him who was 'the Amen, the Faithful and True Witness' (*Rev. 3:14–17*).

Christ may well say of churches today, as God said of the church under the Old Testament, 'I planted you a noble vine, a seed of highest quality. How then have you turned before me into the degenerate plant of an alien vine?' (*Jer. 2:21*). 'How the faithful city has become a harlot! It was full of justice; righteousness lodged in it, but now murderers. Your silver has become dross, your wine mixed with water' (*Isa. 1:21, 22*).

So today in many churches gospel silver has become dross, its pure wine watered down by tradition and reason. Men are so soon weary of gospel truths and are only too willing to exchange them for their own ideas and inventions: 'Has a nation changed its god, which are not gods? But my people have changed their Glory for what does not profit' (*Jer. 2:11*).

THE SPECIAL CLAIM OF THE CHURCH OF ROME

But the Church of Rome claims a special privilege. She does not claim the internal privilege of grace working in the minds and wills of all that belong to her communion, keeping them from falling into error and abandoning true saving faith and obedience, but rather an outward privilege of *indefectibility*.

This gift of indefectibility which Rome claims for herself keeps her infallibly in that state which the gospel requires. She does not know how the gift of indefectibility works, but it does, whether she likes it or not, whether she wills it or not!

This claim to the gift of indefectibility was made by the Jews under the Old Testament: 'The temple of the Lord, the temple of the Lord, the temple of the Lord are these!' (*Jer. 7:4*).

They trusted that because they had the temple of the Lord, God would infallibly keep them from apostasy, however great their sins might be. But Jeremiah declares that they were trusting in lying words: 'Behold, you trust in lying words that cannot profit. Will you steal, murder, commit adultery, swear falsely, burn incense to Baal, and walk after other gods whom you do not know, and then come and stand before me in this house which is called by my name and say, "We are delivered to do all these abominations"?' (*Jer. 7:8–10*).

Peter, alone amongst all the apostles, claimed indefectibility. He alone would not deny Christ when it came to the crunch. But see how indefectible he was! Though all the apostles forsook Christ, only Peter forsook and denied him!

But this claim of indefectibility made by Rome is

accompanied with a special apostasy above all the other churches in the world.

Nothing can be more spurious in itself, nor more pernicious to the souls of men, than this claim when there are no evidences to support but plenty to deny it.

What fierce, bloody and causeless wars have Catholic nations been engaged in. Does this prove that they were ruled by the Prince of peace? What great wickednesses have been committed by the Roman Church, as history plainly shows.

Rome has never in all its history been an example of love and peace, but rather of wars and terrible persecutions. How does her behaviour agree with Isaiah 2:2–4? How does her behaviour agree with Christ's teachings on unity, love and peace?

But if Rome is truly indefectible, then we would expect something better than the desolations she has brought on the earth through the lusts and rage of those who claim to be led by the Holy Spirit of God and to be ruled by Christ, the Prince of peace and love.

Rome in no way represents the kingdom of righteousness, love and peace which Christ came to set up in the world.

Rather than being a kingdom of light, truth and holiness; an example of separation from the world, in principles, desires and behaviour; an example of communion with God and lovingkindness among men; an example of righteousness, joy and peace in the Holy Spirit, history has shown her to be a kingdom of darkness, pride, ignorance, ambition, persecution, blood, superstition and idolatry.

She claims unity, because all Catholics are united under one head, the pope. This is the unity which Rome believes is the only unity required of all Christians. But gospel unity is unity in Christ and submission to his rule.

Rome claims holiness of worship because of the saints that have been among them and the charity of many testified by magnificent works of piety and generosity. But the gospel requires sanctification, holiness and love. It requires conformity to Christ in heavenly-mindedness and obedience. So Rome has a 'form of godliness', but she 'denies its power' (*2 Tim. 3:5*).

The grace of God in the gospel teaches Christians 'to deny all ungodliness and worldly lusts, and to live soberly, righteously and godly in this present world' (*Titus 2:11, 12*). But men renounce these, preferring to be 'foolish, disobedient, deceived, serving various lusts and pleasures, living in malice and envy, hateful and hating one another' (*Titus 3:3*). Such persons know nothing of being saved 'through the washing of regeneration and renewing of the Holy Spirit' (*Titus 3:5*).

When the power of godliness is lost, men resort to the outward appearance in a vain attempt to give credence to their existence. When Shishak, King of Egypt, came up against Jerusalem and took away the gold shields which Solomon had made, King Rehoboam made bronze shields in their place (*1 Kings 14:25–27*).

In the same way, when the majority of members in the Church of Rome lost and denied the power of the gold shields of faith, love, peace, holiness, conformity to Christ, self-denial and all the principles of heavenly behaviour, having lost and despised all the true glory of Christianity, she set up in their place bronze shields, which are only a form or image of that glory. With this form or image, Rome is content, and by this form and image she attempts to deceive others into believing that she alone is the true church of Christ on earth.

Instead of the gold shield of that mystical, spiritual union with Christ which truly unites Christians, and which Christ prayed for and purchased by his blood, Rome has set up the bronze shield of professed subjection to the pope as the only true unity in the church.

Instead of the gold shield of that heavenly *love* for one another in Christ and for his sake by which grace Christ renews the souls of believers, Rome has set up the bronze shield of a profession of outward works of charity and generosity, measured and valued by the rewards which the church of Rome gives in return for these works done for her benefit and worldly enrichment and advancement.

Instead of the gold shield of the Spirit's effective works of grace in the soul, Rome has set up the bronze shield of outward man-made ordinances.

The gold shield of regeneration becomes the bronze shield of baptism. The gold shield of growth in grace becomes the bronze shield of episcopal confirmation. The gold shield of the application by faith of the blood of Christ once offered in that holy sacrifice for us is replaced by the worthless bronze shield of the daily sacrifice of the mass offered for the sins of the living and the dead. The gold shield of spiritual mortification of sin is replaced by the bronze shields of penances and severe, painful bodily punishments. In the place of the gold shield of the Spirit of grace and supplication ruling in worship are set up the bronze shields of man-made liturgies invented and composed by they know not whom.

But worst of all, rejecting the humble, holy, meek, diligent endeavours to keep all true believers in obedience, love, unity and fruitful behaviour by applying the commands of Christ to their souls and consciences through the Spirit and with his authority, Rome has set up a worldly domination over God's heritage using more force, fraud, extortion, oppression, violence and bloodshed than, it may be, has any secular government of any tyrannical state in the world.

ROME'S REPLY TO THESE CRITICISMS

'Whatever criticisms and condemnations you level against us, it doesn't matter, because the promise of the Spirit to lead the church into all truth is not only granted to us but also *confined* to us alone, so that all who are in communion with us are eternally secure as to faith and belief, whatever other evils we may fall into. We alone have the promised Spirit of Christ and that is what makes our church alone indefectible.'

If this is true, then Rome wins the day and no criticisms levelled against her behaviour can detract from her indefectibility.

But her claim is both weak and contemptible. Her argument amounts to no more than this: 'We are the church, therefore the promise of the Spirit is given to us alone.' In other words, they are the church because they say they are the church and therefore they alone must have the promised Holy Spirit.

But if she says, 'We are the church because the promised Spirit has been given to us and to us alone', then the truth of this claim can be more easily tested and a satisfactory conclusion reached.

Where the Spirit is, according to the promise of Christ, there is Christ's true church because 'any who do not have the Spirit of Christ are none of his' (*Rom. 8:9*). And where the Spirit is, he will most surely reveal himself infallibly by his works and by his gifts and graces. He is the Spirit of truth, so the world cannot receive him. So if the Spirit abides only in the communion of the Roman church, then all others who claim to be churches of Christ but who are not in communion with Rome cannot have the Spirit and it would be clearly seen that the Spirit of Christ does not abide with them.

So if Rome can show clearly that she alone enjoys the gracious works of the Spirit, that she alone is furnished and supplied with his gifts, whether extraordinary or ordinary, then her claim to be the only true church of Christ is proved, and she frees herself from any charge of dangerous apostasy which is laid at her doors.

But instead of being led into all truth, Rome has so departed from the truth that scarcely a grain of the true gospel remains in her.

The gospel of Christ is the only outward means of bringing sinners to be reconciled to God. It is the Spirit's only handbook, given to teach men how to walk before God in obedience to his will and to his glory. Scripture has no other use whatever.

So when Rome claims that she alone possesses the truth, that she alone is the true interpreter of Scripture, whether she uses Scripture for its proper purpose or not, and when she tells all who profess subjection to her that she will secure their eternal future – even though they remain ignorant of the gospel and continue to lead sinful lives and remain unreconciled to God, with hearts still at enmity with God – she does nothing but expose the gospel to contempt and ridicule in the eyes of the world.

So, notwithstanding these claims made by Rome, we will proceed to show how the majority of Christians have partially apostatized from the truth of the gospel, and ask why they have done so, how they came to this state of partial apostasy, and what brought them to such apostasy.

3: *Apostasy from the Truth of the Gospel*

The gospel is made up of three things:

(1) There is the mystery of its doctrine. What we are to believe.

(2) There is the holiness of its commands. How we are to live.

(3) There is the purity of its worship. How our professed faith and obedience is tested.

The foundation of true holiness and true Christian worship is the doctrine of the gospel, what we are to believe. So when Christian doctrine is neglected, forsaken or corrupted, true holiness and worship will also be neglected, forsaken and corrupted.

Men may profess the truth and yet not obey it (*Titus 1:16; 2 Tim. 3:5*).

The obedience the gospel requires is the 'obedience of faith' (*Rom. 1:5*). Christians are to be 'obedient to the faith' (*Acts 6:7*). It is 'this grace of God which teaches men to live soberly, righteously and godly in this present world', so as to find acceptance with God (*Titus 2:11, 12*). So when the doctrine of the gospel is neglected or forsaken, then there will be a falling away from true gospel holiness and worship.

Paul declared at the end of his ministry that 'he had kept the faith' (*2 Tim. 4:6–8*). This had been his major concern throughout his whole ministry.

It had not been easy for Paul to 'keep the faith'. It involved severe warfare and conflict. How different was Paul from so many today who think it an easy matter 'to keep the faith'.

It was Paul's great concern that Timothy also should 'keep the faith' (*1 Tim. 6:20, 21; 2 Tim. 1:13, 14*).

Titus was charged by Paul to rebuke those who were prone to neglect or forsake the truth of the gospel for Jewish fables and commands of men (*Titus 1:13, 14*).

Jude calls all Christians to 'earnestly contend for the faith' because many are all too ready to corrupt it and turn away from it (*Jude 3*).

One would think that the first churches, planted by the apostles and taught by them, had the greatest advantage when it came to knowing the mystery and truth of the gospel. The apostles revealed to them 'the whole counsel of God', and withheld nothing that was profitable to them (*Acts 20:18–21, 26, 27*). Their authority was immediately from Christ and they were absolutely infallible in all that they taught. You would have thought, then, that the early churches would have kept the faith pure and not departed from it.

The church in Corinth was planted by Paul and watered by that great evangelist Apollos. Yet, in about five or six years, many in that church had denied the resurrection of the dead (*1 Cor. 15:12–18*).

The churches of the Galatians were also planted by Paul. He instructed them in the whole counsel of God. They treated him as an angel of God, received him as if he were Jesus Christ himself and esteemed him above the sight of their own eyes (*Gal. 4:14, 15*). Yet in a very short while, they fell from the doctrine of grace and justification by faith alone, to seek for righteousness, as it were, by the works of the law. This so amazed Paul that he thought they had been bewitched (*Gal. 3:1*). Notwithstanding the clear demonstration of the truth which they had received, and the power of the word which they had experienced, they suddenly apostatized from it.

So we ought not to think it strange if Christians today fall away so easily from the gospel after having received it.

Paul's letters to Timothy and Titus were full of warnings of the readiness of all sorts of persons to apostatize from the truth. John also in his epistles tells of apostasies from the gospel and warns Christians of the danger of falling away, as does Jude also in his epistle. Nearly all the seven churches mentioned in the Book of Revelation were accused of apostasy by Jesus Christ himself.

So, if apostolic churches easily fell into apostasy even when the apostles were still alive, shall we, who do not have the same advantages as they, cease to be watchful and neglect to use all the means of keeping ourselves from falling away?

And what about the churches that followed, when the sacred records were complete and the apostles were dead?

While he was still alive, Paul warned the elders of the church at Ephesus that 'he knew that after his death, savage wolves would come in among them, not sparing the flock'. He warned them also 'that from among themselves men would rise up, speaking perverse things, to draw away the disciples after themselves' (*Acts 20:29, 30*).

Peter also warned about false teachers who would come among them, secretly bringing in destructive heresies, even denying the Lord who bought them, who would bring on themselves swift destruction. In addition, Peter warned that many would follow their destructive ways, because of whom the way of truth would be blasphemed (*2 Pet. 2:1, 2*).

That Paul's warning to the Ephesian elders was necessary is seen by Christ's judgment on that church later on (*Rev. 2:4, 5*). Paul also gives Timothy salutary warnings of coming apostasy (*2 Tim. 4:1–4; 1 Tim. 4:1, 2*).

The other apostles also warned the churches of approaching apostasy (*Jude 17, 18*). John warns of the coming antichrist (*1 John 4:3*). And Paul warns the Thessalonian Christians of the coming of the 'lawless one' (*2 Thess. 2:3, 5, 6*).

[46]

So the great testimony of the Spirit of God in those days was that the visible church would fall away from the faith, and one of the chief ways by which Satan brought this apostasy about was by getting Christians to believe that this or that church, the Church of Rome, for instance, was infallible and indefectible, and so could never fall away from the faith. By this means, Satan deluded men into rejecting the warnings given by the Spirit, so making Christians feel secure. Because the Spirit's warnings were neglected and forsaken, Christians were deceived into not being watchful. So Christians, believing their church was infallible and indefectible and that it could never fall into apostasy, were easily led into that great apostasy which grew to its greatest height in the Church of Rome. The devil persuaded Christians to believe that apostate teachings were the truth, and so led them to justify the apostasy by the doctrine of indefectibility.

FOUR BASIC WARNINGS GIVEN BY THE SPIRIT:

(1) The first of these warnings was that 'men from among the body of pastors and teachers would arise, teaching perverse things'.

(2) The second warning was that 'savage wolves would enter the church, not sparing the flock'.

(3) The third warning was that people would get tired of hearing sound doctrine, and would turn from the truth to fables.

(4) The fourth warning was that a gradual, secret, mysterious general apostasy would arise in the whole visible church. This was the 'mystery of iniquity'.

All these prophesied warnings came to pass in due time.

(1) Many of the early church Fathers, the principal teachers in the first ages of the church after the apostles, especially among those whose writings have been passed

[47]

down to posterity, neglected the gospel and its simplicity, and instead embraced and taught many perverse things contrary to the gospel which had been committed to them. They did not treat evangelical mysteries with that reverence and godly fear which was their duty. Holding to the fundamental principles of Christianity, they corrupted and debased the pure and holy doctrine of Jesus and his apostles by ingenious speculations, philosophical prejudices and presuppositions, by wrested allegorical expositions and by opinions and ideas contradictory to the Word of God. So the first warning came to pass.

(2) Then into the church came heretics of every kind whom I look on as the 'savage wolves' Paul warned of.

There were those heretics who, regardless of the gospel and with contempt for it, fell away into foolish, extravagant, heathenish imaginations, unintelligible, endless fancies, accompanied for the most part by wicked practices, and although they kept the name of Christian, they completely and totally fell away from Christ and his gospel. Peter prophesied the coming of these heretics (2 Pet. 2:1, 2). Such heretics were the Gnostics, the Marcionites and the Manichees.

There was another sort of heresies and so of real apostasy from the mystery of the gospel, whose authors and followers yet pretended to adhere to the Christian faith and professed themselves to be Christians. These heresies concerned the doctrines of the person and grace of Christ.

The Arians denied Christ's deity. The Pelagians denied his satisfaction, merit and grace.

Arianism was poured out like a flood from the mouth of the old serpent, carrying all before it like a torrent, whilst Pelagianism, like a deadly poison, insinuated itself into the very vitals of the church. But though Arianism has been swept from the church, Pelagianism plays no small part in

[48]

the religion of the majority of Christians today. So the second warning came to pass.

(3) Then men began to grow tired and weary of sound doctrine.

About the third century, monkish fables began to be broached in the world. Instead of preaching the doctrines of grace, of justification by the blood of Christ, of faith and repentance, and of holy obedience, they proclaimed stories of dreams and visions, of angelic perfection in themselves, of self-invented devotions, of uncommanded severities of the body and a thousand other foolish superstitions. By such fables, numberless souls turned from the truth and simplicity of the gospel, despising the whole doctrine of our Lord Jesus Christ and his apostles. These were prophesied of in 1 Timothy 4:1–3. So the third warning came to pass.

(4) The last warning of the Spirit was the secret working of the 'mystery of iniquity'. This was that fatal apostasy brought about by false teachers, savage wolves, weariness of hearing sound doctrine and other numberless deceits of Satan, along with the vanity of the minds and the lusts of the hearts of men. Under this terrible apostasy, the world groaned and by it was ruined. This terrible apostasy rose to its height in the papacy. The pure wine of the gospel was poisoned and the pure worship of the gospel was fearfully corrupted, so that it no longer refreshed the souls of men, but rather being made so bitter, the souls of men, like Christ on the cross, after tasting it, would not drink it.

During this time, the true church was driven into the wilderness, where it was secretly nourished by the Spirit and the Word of God, and the few witnesses who still remained prophesied in sackcloth, and sealed their testimony with their blood (*Rev. 12:11; 11:3, 7, 8*).

Then God graciously visited the remnant of his inheritance and raised up many faithful servants of Christ by whom the work of reformation was successfully begun and carried on in many nations and churches.

That this reformation was truly the work of God is shown by the following truths:

The doctrine of the Reformers was agreeable to Scripture.

The consciences of men were freed from the bondage of fear, superstition and foolish ideas by the truth and directed into the ways of gospel obedience.

Many were granted on behalf of Christ, not only to believe in him but also to suffer for him, sealing their testimony with their blood, which brought many who saw them die out of Romanism into the light of the glorious gospel of Christ.

The fruit which the Reformation bore in many nations by the real conversion of multitudes to God, their spiritual growth and holy obedience, their solid spiritual comfort in life and death, along with many other spiritual blessings, testify that this work was indeed of God.

It cannot be denied that many churches recovered from that mortal disease under whose power they had lain so long. But to reach perfect health and soundness and to prevent a relapse, much care and diligence is required. But instead of going on with the work of reformation until all apostasy had been swept away, the power of the Reformation lost its force and churches, freed from Rome, began to sink back once again into apostasy. So we have another sad evidence of the proneness of men to grow tired of the truths of the gospel after they had been taught them, and for various reasons turned back along the paths of apostasy.

Some return to the Roman Catholic Church, either because its sacramentalism appeals to them as an 'easy' way to deal with their sense of guilt, or because they believe its religion will hide their own sin. There are always those who, like the Israelites, would prefer someone to lead them back to

Egypt rather than through the wilderness to the promised land!

However, since the Reformation, other deviations from the gospel have arisen. Not only has Arminianism influenced many people, but also Socinianism. It had its roots at the time of the Reformation, in the thought of Laelius Socinus, and was promulgated by his nephew Faustus Socinus. Socinianism is, essentially, a rationalistic approach to the Christian faith, making man's fallen reason the measuring stick for belief. Consequently, it denied the Trinity, the incarnation and deity of Jesus Christ and other cardinal doctrines. In whatever guise it appears, it clearly involves a wholescale rejection of the gospel.

Such attacks on genuine Christianty can sometimes weaken the testimony of true believers. It is, therefore, important for us to ask the question: What lies behind such apostasy? To that we will turn in the next chapter.

4: The Reasons and Causes of Apostasy from the Gospel

Turning one's back on the truth of the gospel, after having received it, is a sin of the highest guilt that brings about the most pernicious results.

Under the Old Testament, God frequently complained by his prophets that his people 'had forsaken him' and gone away from him, by which he meant that they had forsaken his doctrine and the institutions of his law which were the means of communion and fellowship between him and his people (*Deut. 28:20; 1 Sam. 8:8; 2 Chron. 34:25; Jer. 5:7, 19; 16:11*).

To convince them of their horrible treatment of him, God asks them to show him what iniquity they had seen in him, what wrong he had done them, how he had so disappointed them that they should grow tired of his laws and worship, rejecting them in favour of false gods and evil ways. That would only bring on them great trouble, both in this world and the next (*Jer. 2:5; Ezek. 18:25*).

If there were nothing in God's laws and worship which was cause for complaint; if they were all holy, just and good; if in the observance of them there was great reward; if by them God did them good and not evil all their days, then there was no excuse for their foolishness and ingratitude.

But those who forsake the doctrines of the gospel, after receiving them and professing openly to be Christ's people, are far worse than the Jews ever were. The guilt of those who turn away from the gospel after receiving it is far greater than the idolatrous revolts of the Jews of old, for the gospel is a clearer revelation of God and much more glorious than that revelation given under the law.

What charges can apostates bring against the gospel to justify their foolishness and ingratitude?

Why, then, do some reject and forsake the gospel after receiving it?

CAUSES AND REASONS FOR APOSTASY FROM THE GOSPEL

Men forsake the gospel because of the rooted enmity in their minds to all spiritual things. 'The carnal mind is enmity against God' (*Rom. 8:7*).

The unconverted mind is not willing to submit to the revelation given to it of the mind and will of God in Christ. The natural, unspiritual man is an 'enemy of the cross of Christ' (*Phil. 3:18*). The natural man 'professes to know God, but in works denies him, being abominable, and disobedient, and disqualified for every good work' (*Titus 1:16*).

When the gospel was first preached, many were convinced of the truth, and received it with joy because it was confirmed by miracles. But their hearts and minds were not in the least reconciled to the doctrines of the gospel (*John 2:23, 24; Acts 8:13*).

After the miracle of feeding the five thousand with five barley loaves and two fish, the people were prepared to receive Christ's doctrine about 'the bread of life that came down from heaven'. They cried out, 'Lord, give us this bread always' (*John 6:34*). But their natural enmity to spiritual things still remained in them. So when Christ began to teach them heavenly mysteries, they immediately began to 'murmur against him', 'quarrelled among themselves' and considered that what he was telling them was a 'hard saying' (*John 6:41, 52, 60*).

Christ gives the reason for their unbelief. They were not

able to receive and believe his teaching until the Father granted it by removing the enmity of their carnal minds and drawing them to Christ (*John 6:64, 65*).

What the crowd thought hard and unintelligible, his disciples understood to be 'the words of eternal life' (*v. 68*).

WHAT EVANGELICAL TRUTHS AIM TO DO IN THE HEARTS OF MEN

The aim of evangelical truths is to get the eyes of men off themselves and their own righteousness for present peace and future glory, and on to Christ and his righteousness. Evangelical truths aim to renew the corrupt minds, wills and desires of sinful men into the image and likeness of God and so to restore men – body, soul and spirit – to a life of wholehearted and holy obedience to God.

But when evangelical truths are pressed on the consciences and practices of men, the enmity in their hearts rises up in rebellion against them.

While the unconverted mind is allowed to play with these truths, speculating and arguing about them, it receives them as something satisfying and pleasing. In fact, it may even be willing to be so guided by these truths as to do many things, yet the unconverted mind still remains on its old foundation of self-sufficiency and self-determination, satisfied that all is under the control of its own free will (*Mark 6:20*).

But when these truths are brought home to their hearts, urging them to renounce faith in themselves, their own self-sufficiency, self-determination and self-righteousness and be renewed in Christ, then that old enmity lurking in their hearts is immediately aroused like some venomous snake ready to strike at the whole gospel. All the lusts of the mind and the flesh; all the deceitful desires of the old nature; all the powers of sin and all carnal and unmortified desires rise up to resist these truths.

So spiritual truths received only in the mind are first neglected, then despised and finally forsaken.

Men, by conviction and for natural reasons and motives, may receive the gospel as truth. But when that truth is applied to their consciences, and the will and desires are called on to repent of their own ways and instead walk in God's ways, then that old enmity rises up and objects.

Evangelical truths are easily received on Arminian terms where that rooted enmity is allowed to retain control over all its decisions, and to be self-sufficient. But when these truths urge man's utter inability to repent and believe without the grace of God first working in them, then that enmity pleads free will, and resists with all its might the sovereignty of God in the salvation of men.

ENMITY AGAINST NATURAL REVELATION

Paul describes the course which the enmity of man takes against natural revelation (*Rom. 1:18–32*).

They could not run away from God's revelation of his eternal power and godhead in creation, because they could not run away from the universe, nor could they run away from themselves as part of God's creation. Not liking to retain the knowledge of God in their minds, they suppressed the truth in unrighteousness (*v. 18*). Instead of worshipping God, they gave themselves up to abominable idolatries and brutish lusts.

ENMITY AGAINST SUPERNATURAL REVELATION

Paul also shows that it is the same with supernatural revelation. The mystery of lawlessness was able to work because men 'did not receive the love of the truth, that they might be saved' (*2 Thess. 2:10*). First, they refused to allow the truth to have any effect on their lives, and then they rejected it for the vilest errors and grossest superstitions.

There are examples of how all sorts of men who have received ideas which are false, vain and foolish, but which are so riveted in their minds by powerful interests and prejudices that not even the most powerful presentation of the truth accompanied by infallible evidences and warnings of the most terrible dangers if they do not repent will prevail on them to renounce their errors. Such examples are seen in false Christians, cults and heresies.

But there are two great examples in history: the Jews and the Church of Rome.

The Jews to this day continue obstinately to hold on to the most irrational unbelief and apostasy from the faith of their father Abraham, in spite of the most terrible hardships and the most horrific disasters which have come on them.

The Church of Rome even to this day clings obstinately to its errors, idolatries, blasphemies and superstitions, even though it abounds with wise and learned men. Even kings and rulers of nations have foolishly subscribed to its errors, impieties, superstitions and idolatries.

No religion can be so foolish or contemptible, but there will always be those clinging tenaciously to it.

Error, once received as truth, takes firmer root in carnal minds than truth ever does or ever can do whilst the mind remains in its unrenewed state. The reason for this is that error is in some way or other suited to the depraved mind, and there is nothing in error that rouses the natural enmity to God and spiritual things rooted in the hearts of men.

The mind, having fallen from truth and goodness, wanders willingly in crooked paths of its own, determining for itself what is good and evil, what is true and what is false (*Eccles. 7:29*).

This is why the 'mystery of iniquity' was so successful in raising up such a great apostasy, which reached its height in the Church of Rome.

[56]

The danger of apostasy will always be present if men receive the truth only in their minds, but do not love it in their hearts and gladly submit to it in their wills. Unless this enmity is conquered and cast out; unless the mind is freed from its depravity; unless the truth works powerfully and effectively upon the heart and soul; unless the truth is learned 'as it is in Jesus', so that men 'put off their previous behaviour, the old man, which is corrupt and filled with deceitful lusts, and are renewed in the spirit of their mind, and put on the new man which in the image of God is created in righteousness and true holiness'; unless they love the truth and value it for the spiritual peace, power and freedom of spirit it brings them, they will fall away in time of persecution and forsake the gospel for other things.

This enmity of heart is the first cause and reason why so many fall away from the doctrine of the gospel after receiving it.

The only way to prevent this falling away from the gospel is to love the truth and to experience its power in the heart.

True religion may be established by law and supported and defended by those in authority, but unless this enmity is rooted out of the hearts of men and love for it is planted there instead, there is no real defence against apostasy.

How is it that after so glorious a Reformation, men should once again relapse into popery?

What will prevent popery returning once again to blight this nation and other nations in the world?

Will severe laws prohibiting its return do it? Never. Anyway, severe laws with terrifying sanctions are never to the glory of true religion.

Will books, written to confute its errors, do it? Never. Few will read them and take them seriously.

The only thing that will do it is the effectual communication of the knowledge of the truth of the gospel to the hearts of men by the Holy Spirit. Evangelical doctrine must be understood by the mind, loved by the heart, and willingly and gladly submitted to by the will (*Rom. 6:17*). Only when the power and love of the truth is implanted in the hearts of the people will popery be driven from our land once again.

Unless men know the true value of the gospel and what great good the gospel brings to them if they receive it in their hearts and live it out in their lives, it is stupid to think that any will remain faithful to it. When difficulties arise, they will say, 'It is foolish to serve God in this way. What profit is there in keeping his ordinances?'

But when God, by the gospel, 'shines in the hearts of men to give them the light of the knowledge of his glory in the face of Jesus Christ'; when they find their consciences freed from the intolerable yoke of superstition and tradition, and that by the word of truth which they have received, they are born again to the living hope of eternal life, their inner man being renewed and their lives transformed; that their hope of immortality is well founded on it, they will, by the grace and strength of the Spirit, abide in the truth to the end of their lives whatever may befall them.

No mere outward form of true religion will stand before the advances of Romish apostasy.

Only the faithful preaching of the gospel – with such an example of zeal and holiness in those by whom it is preached, winning the hearts of the people to the evangelical truths proclaimed, begetting in all who hear such a delight in them that they willingly submit to Christ and trust in him alone for salvation, proving by holy obedience to his will that the word has indeed been powerfully implanted in their hearts – will halt the insidious advances of Romish apostasy.

This is the only way which God has ordained and which he blesses (*Acts 20:32*).

'But surely the apostles were at a greater advantage than us because they were equipped with extraordinary gifts, whereas we only have ordinary gifts?'

The apostles had extraordinary gifts because they were called to do an extraordinary work. We are only called to an ordinary work, so the Spirit only equips us with ordinary gifts. But the Holy Spirit can make his ordinary gifts equally effective as his extraordinary gifts. It was not the miracles that rooted out the enmity in men's hearts and implanted a true repentance and faith, but the regenerating work of the Holy Spirit. Christ did many mighty miracles, yet they still did not believe in him (*John 12:37*).

Paul tells young Timothy that the time would come when sound doctrine would no longer be tolerated. Because of this, men would appoint teachers who would preach only what the people wanted to hear, and as a result they would be turned away from the truth to fables (*2 Tim. 4:3, 4*).

What, then, was Timothy to do to prevent this happening?

Paul says, 'I charge you therefore before God and the Lord Jesus Christ, who will judge the living and the dead at his appearing and his kingdom: preach the word! Be ready in season and out of season. Convince, rebuke, exhort, with all longsuffering and teaching. Be watchful in all things, endure afflictions, do the work of an evangelist, fulfil your ministry' (*2 Tim. 4:1, 2, 5*). This is the ordinary work to which we are called and for which the Spirit equips us with ordinary gifts.

So Paul describes those who were evangelically converted to God as those who 'were slaves of sin', yet who obeyed from the heart that form of doctrine to which they were delivered, and having been set free from sin, they had become slaves of righteousness (*Rom. 6:17, 18*).

Firstly, by the use of force

The Church of Rome, both in the preservation of its religion and also in the advancement of it in the world, has always advocated the use of force. But how can Christians be at peace, rejoicing in God through Jesus Christ, whilst they bring terror, persecution, ruin and destruction on others merely for the defence of their religion? Did Christ the Prince of peace advocate force for the preservation and advancement of his religion in the world?

Secondly, by accommodating religion to the sinful lusts and corruptions of men

The apostate church allows men to continue to sin, but at the same time to give the appearance of being truly Christian.

Natural men are alienated from God and enemies of God in their minds, doing wicked works (*Col. 1:21*). 'Their understanding is darkened, being alienated from the life of God, because of the ignorance that is in them because of the hardness of their heart, who being past feeling, having given themselves over to licentiousness, to work all uncleanness with greediness' (*Eph. 4:18–19*).

With such love of sin and with rooted enmity towards God and his gospel, men cannot but secretly hate the truth.

They love darkness rather than light (*John 3:19, 20*). They love the praise of men more than the praise of God (*John 12:42, 43*). They may appear to receive the truth, but they do not love the truth (*2 Thess. 2:10*).

Paul warns Timothy that 'in the last days perilous times will come, for men will be lovers of themselves, lovers of money, boasters, proud, blasphemers, disobedient to parents, unthankful, unholy, unloving, unforgiving, slanderers, without self-control, brutal, despisers of good, traitors, headstrong, haughty, lovers of pleasure rather than lovers of God, having a form of godliness but denying its power'. 'From such', says Paul, 'turn away'.

So either the church had to obey this apostolic command, or it had to accommodate itself to their lusts.

The great secret purpose of sinful man is to go on living his sinful life with as little trouble as possible in the present life, and with every hope of avoiding future punishments in the next.

There are two ways of doing this:

(1) *Deny that there is a God.* Obliterate all ideas of good and evil, and all sense of future rewards and punishments (*Psa. 14:1; 10:4*).

But it is difficult to be an atheist, because that which may be known of God is evident in them (*Rom. 1:19,* margin). The atheist cannot run away from the truth of God because he cannot run away from himself, and nor can he run away from the evidences of God's eternal power and godhead in all creation (*Rom. 1:20*). Neither can the atheist free himself from the knowledge of God's judgments (*Rom. 1:32*). So the outward boasting of the atheist is a sorry plaster for his inward fears.

(2) *Give them a religion which will allow men to continue to indulge their sinful lusts and yet still appear to be Christian* (*2 Tim. 3:5*).

Sin and conscience must be brought to live peaceably with each other. Sin resists conscience and conscience resists sin so that there can be no peace while both exist. But corrupt nature will bring them to live peaceably together (*2 Pet. 2:18, 19*).

The first thing that must be done is to remove the lion of regeneration and the renovation of the corrupt nature into the image and likeness of God, which deters many from entering into true religion. So the outward ordinance of baptism replaces the inward regenerating work of the Holy Spirit.

The next thing that must be done is to provide a substitute

for the internal sanctification of the whole person, the spiritual mortification of sin and wholehearted obedience, so that conscience will be satisfied, but that sin might continue to reign and be indulged.

So absolutions, daily masses, indulgences and – if the worst comes to the worst – purgatory enable the sinner to remain unrepentant and at the same time remove fear of future punishments. Confessions, penances and the giving of alms enable men to continue to live in their sins and at the same time to pacify their consciences.

This is the reason why so many return to the Romish apostasy after having received the knowledge of the gospel. It is because in that church that conscience can be pacified and men left to continue in their sinful ways in peace.

5: *Darkness and Ignorance a Cause of Apostasy*

The purpose of the gospel is to bring the minds of men out of the darkness of error into the light of the knowledge of God in the face of Jesus Christ (*2 Cor. 4:6*).

The sad fact is that there is a spiritual darkness on the minds of men by nature. In order, then, to discern spiritual things, spiritual illumination is needed. Where this spiritual illumination is, there the darkness of error is dispelled. The purpose of light is to dispel darkness. So spiritual darkness must be acknowledged as part of man's depravity or the gift and grace of God's illumination must be rejected. The great proof of spiritual darkness is seen in man's denial of any need of spiritual light. Nevertheless, though unrecognized by the spiritually blind, spiritual illumination is the gift of him who 'commanded light to shine out of darkness' (*2 Cor. 4:6*).

There is a glory and beauty in the spiritual truths of the gospel which cannot be seen by the unspiritual man. In the spiritual truths of the gospel 'the wisdom of God in a mystery' is revealed (*1 Cor. 2:6, 7*). This wisdom has many features and it is beyond the ability of the human mind to discover it (*Eph. 3:10; 1 Cor. 2:9, 10*).

In the truths of the gospel are to be seen the divine glory and excellence of God's wisdom itself, and as revealed in the person and grace of Christ. The purpose of God's wisdom revealed in all its glory in the gospel is the renewal of our nature into God's image by the divine life of faith and obedience.

But none of these spiritual doctrines can be understood or spiritually discerned without the Spirit's work of illumination. Man may know the doctrines in his mind only, yet, still being under the power of spiritual darkness, cannot discern their spiritual nature and glory. The proof of this is to be seen in all the prayers of holy men in Scripture for spiritual light and teaching; in all God's promises to savingly enlighten men; and in descriptions of his illuminating work. Whoever has spiritual insight and knowledge of these things has certainly experienced this illumination and his mind will be and is certainly being transformed into their image (*2 Cor. 3:18*).

Without this illumination, the mind has no stable foundation and no lasting strength and ability to abide in the truth against temptation, opposition and deceivers, because it has no solid assurance of the truth of these things.

Assurance from outward, natural understanding of spiritual things is impossible, nor can unenlightened reason prove to our minds that these truths are from God.

To be fully assured that these truths are given to us by God will enable us to stand firm against temptations and opposition. But this assurance arises only from a sight of them given to us by the Holy Spirit. But once their reality and power are experienced in our minds, we are fully persuaded of their divine origin and truth and this will enable us to resist all temptations to fall away from them.

This involves renewal of our minds by spiritual enlightenment and faith; the embracing of these things by the will as truths to be known and believed and that with a holy, heavenly, unconquerable love, and the constant approval and praise of them as the good, acceptable and perfect will of God in all things. This assurance, given to us by spiritual illumination, is much greater than could ever be given us by natural understanding and reason, and so, in Scripture, is much to be preferred.

LACK OF SPIRITUAL ILLUMINATION A REASON WHY SO MANY
FALL AWAY FROM EVANGELICAL TRUTHS

How did men under the papal apostasy gradually desert the
chief truths of the gospel and all the spiritual glory of its
worship? They did so because they had no spiritual discern-
ment of the divine glory and beauty of evangelical truths and
no experience of their power on their minds. So they chose
those things whose outward, painted beauty they could see.

Many who were learned and skilled in the doctrines of the
gospel, who were seen as pillars of the truth, have yet
apostatized, falling into Arianism, Pelagianism, Socinianism
and Popery.

Two truths for the comfort of believers

Some true believers, seeing great men of the gospel falling
away into apostasy, fear that they may well do the same. So
for their comfort the following two truths must be held:

(1) God has chosen a people in Christ from before the
foundation of the world. These he has given to Christ,
entrusting him with their complete and full salvation. Thus
God's purpose is to preserve his elect and to keep them from
ever falling away from him. Jesus said, 'This is the will of the
Father who sent me, that of all he has given me I should lose
nothing, but should raise it up at the last day. And this is the
will of him who sent me, that everyone who sees the Son and
believes in him may have everlasting life; and I will raise him
up at the last day' (*John 6:39, 40*).

(2) God intends to preserve his elect in holiness. 'The
Lord knows those who are his' and 'Let everyone who names
the name of Christ depart from iniquity' (*2 Tim. 2:19*).

No-one who forsakes the truth has ever seen the glory of it
or has ever experienced its power (*1 John 2:19; Heb. 6:9*).
Without the saving illumination of the truth by the Holy
Spirit, we have no assurance that we will always 'quit
ourselves like men' and 'stand fast in the faith'.

Scepticism

Without spiritual illumination, the doctrines of the gospel are open to scepticism. Sceptics pretend not to renounce or forsake the truth. But they talk about the truth and argue about it with a 'take it or leave it' attitude about them. They are indifferent as to whether it is true or not. Scripture, the Trinity, Christ and his offices, justification by grace and all the other great truths of the gospel are weighed and examined in the defiled, tottering scales of bold, irreverent sceptical discussions. They may be teachers of religion, but they show their ignorance of the fundamental difference between truth and error. They cannot see the glory, beauty and power of truth, so it is all one to them whether it is truth or whether it is error.

Spiritual, heavenly truth is related to the being and infinite wisdom, goodness, love and grace of God. Therefore, it has all these divine characteristics impressed upon it which makes it glorious, lovely and utterly desirable to those able to see these divine evidences.

Error, on the other hand, being related to Satan as head of the original apostasy, is distorted, deformed and confusing to the mind.

Truth has the power to transform the soul into the image of God and to fill it with love for the truth and with the power to obey the truth.

Error, on the other hand, turns the mind aside to crooked paths of foolishness and superstition, or of pride and self-advancement.

Were men aware of this practical difference between truth and error, they would give up their scepticism, speculation and indifference to truth and search for it in its life and power.

Truth, truly known, will beget reverence, love and sacred esteem in the souls of men, so that they would not dare to prostitute it to scepticism or allow it to be bandied about by every foolish imagination.

Darkness keeps the mind and soul from arriving at any assurance of the truth; it prevents the soul from loving the truth and so provides no defence for the person against apostasy. Each man, in his ignorance of what is truth and what is error, is left to determine what is truth for himself. But each man has his own idea and opinion of what truth is. So with every man's opinion equally as valid as every other man's opinion, it becomes easy to wander from truth to error, which is the way of scepticism.

In this way, truth was lost and people gradually wandered into the papal apostasy. Today, multitudes are ready to go the same way.

Truth is the only guide to right thinking. If the mind is not guided by truth, its thoughts will soon wander into error.

Divine truth is the only guide of the mind in all its thoughts about God. Without divine revelation, man will never have right thoughts about God.

Many who accept divine truths with their minds, even in its greatest purity and highest revelations, are often just as wicked and just as unholy in their lives as are those who are led by error and superstition. The lives of many Protestants are no better and often much worse than the lives of Papists, Jews and Muslims. Sometimes, Papists, Muslims and Jews, whose minds are led by errors and superstitions, are often more charitable, more generous, more zealous in mortifying the flesh and in self-denial than many Protestants who profess to have truly received the gospel.

All false religions claim that their followers are more holy in their lives than those who hold to the gospel of Christ. This is their argument when they wish to win converts to themselves.

Therefore, the lives of those who profess to hold to the

[67]

truth are not the criteria for judging what is truth and what is error. But where truth has a powerful hold of the mind, then the life will more perfectly reflect its glory and beauty for all to see.

But let it be known that he is no firm, stable Christian, able to resist all temptations to apostasy, who has not received the truth as a result of the Spirit's illumination of his mind, and who has not experienced the power of its transforming influence in his life. A true Christian is not unwilling that what he believes be impartially judged by his life, not looking for perfection, which he does not claim in this world, but for sincerity.

But if lives are to be the judge of truth, then at times error will carry the day.

The gospel will not transform minds unless it first communicates those spiritual principles which are necessary if its work of transforming the mind is to be effective. Put new wine into old bottles and all is lost, bottles and wine also. Put the doctrine of the gospel into an old, unrenewed, corrupt sceptical mind, and it is soon polluted and spoiled, and because it is unable to produce holiness of life, turns the mind in scepticism against it.

Many have seen how ineffectual it is to put gospel mysteries into carnal men and so have abandoned preaching them, sticking only to those doctrines which are suited to the natural understanding of men, such as moral behaviour and obedience to the law.

The holiness which the gospel requires is the transformation of our souls into the image and likeness of God. This is the new nature which gladly submits to the 'good and acceptable and perfect will of God' (*Rom. 12:2*). But this will not happen unless we can 'behold the glory of the Lord', for by that alone can we be 'changed into the same image from glory to glory' (*2 Cor. 3:18*). Nor can we 'behold that glory', unless 'he who commanded the light to shine out of darkness shines in our hearts to give us the knowledge of it' (2 Cor. 4:6). This is why the doctrine of the gospel is ineffective in the hearts and lives of many by whom its truth is openly acknowledged and professed.

The advantages of false religion

The motives of false religion to bring about reformation of lives and to drive them to their duties are all suited to natural understanding or to the superstitions, fears, desires, pride and other depraved feelings.

Motives which the natural mind can understand are many. Heathen philosophers of old sought to get their followers to improve the 'natural light' in them. Obedience to the law is also urged, but not the purity of the moral law which demands the obedience of the heart, but only outward morality which must meet the demands of the traditions of men. These traditions make void the law by lowering its demands and replacing it with the lesser demands of tradition. These natural motives are found in all false religions, including false Christian sects and cults.

Other motives, especially among Romanists, are such doctrines as the attainment of merit, satisfactions for sin, confessions, penances and finally purgatory. All these things arouse a feeling of awe in men's minds and so have some influence on their lives which gospel principles and motives could not produce. Obedience and subjection to Romish principles and motives often lead to the appearance of great acts of devotion, great outward works of goodness and charity, great austerities and great self-renunciations.

Why, then, does the truth of the gospel not produce glorious works of obedience in all by whom it is received and professed?

The disadvantages of truth

Truth is more excellent than error. Heavenly light is more excellent than superstition. Faith is more excellent than

[69]

fearful terrors of invented, imaginary torments. True peace is more excellent than outward reputation and glory.

There is a holiness, a fruitfulness in good works, which is wrought, preserved and maintained by the truth of the gospel in those who are truly regenerated and sanctified by the Holy Spirit, who receive the power of truth in their minds and souls. This holiness is quite different from that produced by all the principles and motives of false religions, which are designed to suit the depraved lusts of men's minds.

But where men are ignorant of the power of the gospel to regenerate and renew their minds, their lives may be as bad as, and it is a great wonder they are not worse than, those of the Papists and of all false sects and cults or of all heathen religions.

False religions have many superstitions and false principles which to some extent restrain sinful lusts and which motivate to praiseworthy deeds.

But nominal Christians, knowing nothing of the power of gospel truth in their lives, cannot please God and cannot live true, holy lives. It is not merely the outward profession of the truth but the inward power of it that is useful to the world and the souls of men.

So that preaching which motivates people by things which natural understanding can grasp and accept, such as outward obedience to the moral laws, is more effective than the declaration of the mysteries of the gospel. The natural man is in the dark when it comes to understanding the mysteries of the gospel because he cannot see their glory, nor experience their power. Nevertheless, the spiritual motives which the gospel reveals are the only true motives of acceptable obedience in God's sight. They and they alone are 'the power of God unto salvation to everyone that believes' (*Rom. 1:16, 17*).

If, then, we want to be established in the truth; if we want to stand fast in the faith; if we want to be kept by the power of

God from all danger of apostasy, then it must be our chief work to have a true, spiritual knowledge of the truth of the gospel and experience the power of it in our lives. Mere notional ideas of the truth, merely having a head knowledge of its doctrines enabling us to talk about them or discuss them with others, will not preserve us from apostasy. And although this spiritual illumination is the gift of God's grace promised to us, yet we are still to seek for it or we shall not have it (*Matt. 7:7–11*).

If we would be sure of not falling away into apostasy, then we must take heed to the following principles:

We must pray earnestly for the Spirit of truth to lead us into all truth (1 Cor. 2:9–12; Eph. 1:16–20; 3:14–19; Col. 2:1–3).

We must make sure that we have learned the truth 'as it is in Jesus' (Eph. 4:20–24).

To learn the truth as it is in Jesus is to experience its transforming power in our lives, mortifying sin, renewing our natures and conforming us into the image of God in righteousness and true holiness.

The whole purpose of the revelation of the mind and will of God in Scripture is that it may work in us a spiritual, practical power, so that we may do the things revealed to us. Where this is not understood and so neglected, men content themselves with a bare, speculative understanding of the gospel and end up rejecting 'the counsel and wisdom of God' in them.

We must learn to esteem a little knowledge which gives true understanding of salvation and sanctification more highly than the highest ideas and speculations of the mind, even though gilded by the reputation of skill, cleverness, eloquence, wit and learning. He who has learned to be meek, humble, lowly, patient, self-denying, holy, zealous, peaceable, seeking purity of heart and desiring to lead a useful life, is indeed the one who is best acquainted with evangelical truth. So let this knowledge be esteemed above all that proud, presumptuous, puffed-up head knowledge which seeks only to get a great reputation for itself in the world.

Do not be satisfied until you have discovered by personal experience the goodness, excellence and beauty in spiritual things. Do not be satisfied until you have embraced these truths with unconquerable love and delight. Without this, your faith is no better than the faith of devils (*James 2:19*).

IGNORANCE, ANOTHER CAUSE OF APOSTASY

Men may know in their heads the doctrines of the Bible, but be ignorant of their divine origin and have no experience of the power of those doctrines in their lives. Others are ignorant of the doctrines of Scripture themselves because they are lazy and will not make any effort to know them. Others are ignorant of the doctrines of Scripture because they have been taught by false teachers (*Prov. 29:18*). If the teachers are blind and the people are blind, then they will both end up in the ditch of eternal hell. Others are ignorant because they have rejected the knowledge of the gospel (*Hos. 4:6*).

Men may, at times of great preaching, appear to receive the truth. Many under the Old Testament, in the time of Josiah's reformation, turned to the profession of the true religion, but 'they did not do it with their whole hearts, but only in pretence' (*Jer. 3:10*). They did it hypocritically.

The first conversion of the world was by the preaching of the apostles, evangelists and others, accompanied by miracles, signs and wonders, great holiness of life and patience under persecutions. None were received or admitted into the Christian religion, except those who were personally convinced of its truth, instructed in its mysteries, conformed to its commands and faithful in face of persecution.

But later on, kings, rulers or potentates, being taught by popes and other princes of the church, became Christian in opposition to paganism. Their allies, kindred and subjects usually followed them into the church. These knew little more of Christianity than its external rites and that it had substituted new saints for old idols.

By this means, their profession of Christianity was laid in profound ignorance of the principles of its most important doctrines and the duties of the gospel. So it became most easy for those who were looked on as guides to lead them into all those foolish doctrines, idolatrous practices, superstitions, devotions and blind subjection to the priests of the church, from which came the fatal apostasy which culminated in the Church of Rome. Knowing but little of what they ought to have known, and not caring to live in holy obedience to what they did know, they willingly embraced those errors and superstitions to which God judicially gave them up. These were the 'strong delusions' which turned them wholly from the gospel (*2 Thess. 2:11*).

In the same way, the majority of this nation received the Protestant religion as the best alternative to Popery. But through negligence and carelessness, sloth, ignorance, laziness and a 'take it or leave it' attitude to the gospel, multitudes are now shamefully ignorant of the rudiments and principles of true religion.

Can anyone who knows anything of the gospel, or of the nature of man's inability to discern spiritual truths, suppose that the reading of prayers and the preaching of a sermon without zeal, life, power or a compassion for souls, accompanied with a light, foolish, worldly behaviour, was how the apostles laid the foundation of the church and then built men up to spiritual perfection by their continual instruction?

From this neglect, 'darkness covered the earth, and gross darkness the people'. Some will not learn. Some have none to teach them. And some are filled with worldly lusts, being lovers of pleasure more than lovers of God.

[73]

This was what made it easy for the papal apostasy to arise. Religion was accommodated to carnal, superstitious minds, leading them all into errors and fables, for they were blind and did not know where they were going. So the important truths of the gospel were abandoned for monkish dreams, legends of foolish, lying miracles and other heathenish superstitions.

It was ignorance that led people to give themselves up to deceivers. This enabled the architects of the Romish apostasy to accommodate their ideas, ways and practices to fit in with the worldly interests of those whom they would seduce into their apostate church.

So, when men are ignorant of true religion, especially of its chief doctrines and the rock foundation on which they rest, they behave like the Samaritans of old who worshipped 'they knew not what' (*John 4:22*). As a result, they are in no way able to defend themselves against the deceits thrust upon them.

John tells us the means of keeping ourselves from apostasy. We must be taught the truth by the Spirit of truth (*1 John 2:19, 20, 27*).

Many are deceived by 'good words and fair speeches' (*Rom. 16:18*). So Paul tells us to grow up to spiritual maturity (*1 Cor. 14:20; 6:2; Heb. 5:14*). We must not be spiritually weak and ignorant (*Eph. 4:14*).

Rome sends out her papal emissaries, wolves in sheep's clothing. Their aim is to overthrow Protestantism, especially in our nation. But how many Protestants would be able to refute the Romanists and defend their faith against them? Protestants are for ever going to church but never coming to the assurance of the truth.

Rome hypnotizes ignorant Protestants by her claims to be the true expression of the Christian faith because it existed before Protestantism and from the days of the apostles.

Before Protestantism brought confusion, disorder and divisions, Rome existed in perfect unity. Romish priests have been granted power to pardon all sorts of sins. Saints, angels and the blessed virgin herself extend mercy, grace and goodness to all Catholics. Daily miracles are wrought in the Roman Church, especially the miracle of transubstantiation in the daily masses throughout the world. Then there are the wonderful examples of holy devotion in the lives of many Catholics. With these and other Romish glories, Rome succeeds in bewitching many ignorant Protestants into believing that Popery is the more excellent way.

Unspiritual, unconverted Protestants cannot understand the great truths of the gospel. They are 'strange things to them'. They cannot understand them. They find Romanism more conducive to their natural, unspiritual, unconverted, worldly minds.

Romanism is ideally suited to the fleshly, carnal, unspiritual man. But the gospel of God and its true spiritual worship is boring and unintelligible to the unspiritual man.

Another deceit is that religion which gets men to look to the 'natural light' that is within them. The natural man finds by experience that there is a light within him, for within all men there is the light of conscience (*Rom. 2:14, 15*). Not experiencing the true illumination of the Holy Spirit, they suppose the natural light of conscience is what is meant by these deceivers, and so are led astray by vague impulses and funny internal feelings, supposing them to be the voice of God speaking directly to them.

Apostasy from a traditional acceptance of truths not understood is easy. How many have perished for lack of knowledge!

Spiritually ignorant Protestants, holding to the traditional Protestant doctrines but knowing nothing of the power of those doctrines in their lives, can and do persecute Romanists, reviling and treating them with contempt, just as much as

Romanists persecute Protestants, reviling and treating them also with contempt. But if these Protestants are called to give a reason for the hope that is within them, they are utterly lost for words. Such Protestants are in great danger of apostasy and may well end up in Rome.

Ignorant preachers and teachers wickedly deliver their people, bound hand and foot, to the power of their spiritual adversaries. On the other hand, faithful, enlightened preaching and regular, faithful instruction in the chief doctrines of the Christian faith is a sure defence against apostasy.

Outward laws, observance of external forms and cere-monies are no defence against apostasy.

Instruction in the truth and spiritual illumination are the means which God has provided for preserving his people from falling away into apostasy and are the only sure defence against the advances of Popery. Either we are in earnest or we do not believe that regular instruction in the truths of the gospel is the only way of keeping people from returning to the Romish apostasy.

The Reformation brought people out of spiritual darkness into the spiritual light of the gospel. Now neglect of teaching those same great truths has brought the people back to spiritual darkness, a ready prey for Popery.

Paul's charge to Timothy is one that every minister ought to heed and take to heart (*2 Tim. 4:1–5*).

Preachers are to be ready to preach at any time. They are to convince, rebuke and exhort with all patience and with faithful teaching. They must not give up even when their hearers will no longer endure sound doctrine but are only too willing to listen to fables.

Paul is telling Timothy that the gospel ministry is hard labour. There is no rest from 'labouring in the word and doctrine of the gospel', backed up by holy living. For the faithful Christian minister there is only constant, endless toil and labour.

Romish ministry, on the other hand, is easy. It is easy for the Romish priest to keep the people in the Romish fold. Their clergy are free to pursue and use the pleasures and honours of this world. They are not obliged to all that irksome labour and endless, painful toil. In fact, the more ignorant their people are, the easier it is to keep them in subjection to the authority of the priests.

If Rome is to be kept at bay, then every Christian needs to grow in spiritual understanding, built up in the knowledge of the mysteries of the gospel and so brought to perfect understanding of the whole counsel of God, especially the purpose of his love and grace in Christ Jesus, so that he is able to be used by the Spirit for the 'saving of souls'.

As ministers, it will be our wisdom to be led and taught by the Holy Spirit. The more exactly our preaching agrees with the gospel, and the less it is mixed with human ideas and speculations, the more difficult it is to instruct men in the knowledge of it.

The minds of carnal, unspiritual men are far more apt and able to understand and remember fables, errors and superstitions than evangelical truths. The former are natural to the depraved mind. But the latter, because of the enmity of the depraved mind to God and to the things of God, it dislikes and utterly rejects, unless that enmity is removed by the grace of God.

So unconverted men will grow more quickly in four or five days in the errors of a false religion than others will do in as many years in the knowledge of the truths of the gospel.

We may have well-grown Papists in a month, who are expert in the mysteries of popish devotion. But progress and growth in the truth and mysteries of the gospel is slow.

Therefore, special diligence and constant watchfulness is needed when instructing the people in spiritual truths or else they will be left an easy prey to the Romish apostasy.

6: *Pride, Neglect and Worldliness, Causes of Apostasy*

The work of the gospel is to 'cast down arguments and every high thing that exalts itself against the knowledge of God, bringing every thought into captivity to the obedience of Christ' (*2 Cor. 10:4, 5*).

The mind of man since the fall is naturally filled with high thoughts of itself. Man thinks he has sovereign free will over all his actions (*Psa. 12:4*). No-one, not even God, can be Lord over them and their future destiny. Nothing is or can be or ought to be required of man but what he is able to understand, obey or do. This freedom of will and self-determination has been pleaded for in all ages of the church under various supposedly Christian doctrines.

The true state of all arguments between the powers of the natural man on the one hand and sovereign grace on the other is as follows. On the one hand, the minds and wills of men are asserted to be self-sufficient. Man is, of his own ability, able to choose aright and to do aright everything necessary for eternal blessedness. On the other hand, man has no sufficiency of himself, but all his sufficiency for eternal blessedness is of God (*2 Cor. 3:5; 9:8*).

The mind of man exalts itself to be its own self-determiner, rule and guide. Man determines for himself what is good and what is evil, what is truth and what is error.

The corrupt mind exalts its own ideas. It loves, applauds, dotes on and firmly embraces its own ideas and opinions. This is the origin of all heresy. This has given birth, growth and progress to every sort of error (*Eccles. 7:29*). Determining for itself truth and error in all spiritual and religious matters is the chief and most pernicious result of the fall from that state of uprightness in which God created us and our minds.

The corrupt mind exalts itself as the sole and absolute judge of God's Word. The corrupt mind determines for itself whether God's Word is true or false, good or evil, to be received or rejected without any supernatural guidance or help. And whatever the mind rejects as not in agreement with its own ideas and system of logic is scorned and despised.

To the corrupt mind the gospel comes with the stamp of God's authority on it, bearing his image and superscription. Divine wisdom, goodness, grace, holiness and power are so impressed on its doctrines that it shows itself clearly to be the 'glorious gospel of the blessed God' (*1 Tim. 1:11*). So it ought to be received with holy respect, with due recognition of its divine origin and glory and as God's voice speaking from heaven. So the writer of the Epistle to the Hebrews warns us not to 'refuse him who speaks. For if they did not escape who refused him who spoke on earth, much more shall we not escape if we turn away from him who speaks from heaven' (*Heb. 12:25*).

Unless it is seen as from God, the gospel will not be received, truly understood or steadfastly believed. The gospel is to be received, 'not as the words of men but as it is in truth, the word of God' (*1 Thess. 2:13*).

The gospel must be received with that submission and subjection of soul and conscience which we who are nothing but dust and ashes should give to the great and holy God (*Gen. 18:27*).

So Jesus says, 'Except you be converted and become as little children you will in no wise enter the kingdom of heaven.'

Unless we deny ourselves and all our own ideas and opinions, unless we become humble and teachable, we can never receive the gospel. God promises to teach the humble and meek (*Psa. 25:9, 14; Isa. 28:9; Psa. 131:2*). A proud spirit greatly hinders the learning of God's Word. The Word of God is a troublesome inmate to an unhumbled mind and heart.

The Word of God is corrupted by men who have carnal confidence in themselves and their own wisdom to understand and interpret it aright.

The gospel is not contrary to reason, but is above reason. Corrupt reason will not accept this truth and so does not accept anything it cannot understand or believe.

In the gospel, there are divine mysteries revealed, which we may understand, but the nature of the divine mysteries themselves we cannot understand. Man's reason is finite, limited and bounded, so it cannot perfectly understand things which infinite wisdom has devised (*Job 11:7–9*). Reason must humbly submit to, and willingly learn from, divine revelation.

In the gospel, there are also things which corrupt reason rejects because it does not like them. The whole of man, including his mind and reason, is impaired, depraved and corrupted, and as Christ came to restore man in his totality, he came also to restore and repair man's mind and reason.

Corrupt reason is unable to discern and judge spiritual matters rightly, so it is apt to invent its own interpretations according to its own prejudices and presuppositions, contrary to what the gospel teaches and requires. It is, therefore, the purpose of the gospel to bring man's reason into captivity to the obedience of faith.

Reason as finite and limited

The gospel requires man to believe things above the ability of reason to judge or discover. It requires man to believe things merely on the authority of divine revelation (*1 Cor. 2:9, 10*). But corrupt reason deems the things of God to be foolishness (*1 Cor. 1:18–25*).

[81]

Some today exalt reason as the true and rightful judge of all divine revelations. Nothing must be accepted except that which agrees with reason. What is above the understanding of reason must be rejected. Thus reason makes itself infinite and unlimited and the wisdom and understanding of God finite and limited.

As there are many things in the gospel which are absolutely above the reach of man's finite reason, it cannot judge them. It can only be the servant of faith in witnessing to them (*1 Cor. 2:11*).

To affirm that we can be obliged to believe no more than we can understand, or that we may reject everything that is above reason's ability to grasp and understand on the supposition that it is against reason, is to renounce the gospel and all divine revelation.

Reason as corrupted and depraved

Corrupt, depraved reason will not receive commands and laws which are contrary to its lusts and inclinations. Depraved reason always seeks to justify itself by good works. But the covenant of grace and justification by faith alone without works are contrary to depraved reason and so it deems them to be unreasonable and so to be rejected (*Rom. 11:6; 8:7*).

As for natural duties of obedience, the gospel teaches that even these are not acceptable to God except by the mediation of Christ and the grace and strength of the Holy Spirit. But this, being contrary to corrupt reason which is self-righteous, it rejects as unreasonable and so not true. The duties of the gospel reason agrees with, but that these duties cannot be done acceptably except through Christ and by the help of the Holy Spirit it utterly and finally rejects.

Reason also judges the gospel by the traditions of its sect or party. Anything that does not agree with the traditions of the sect or party which reason upholds is to be rejected.

[82]

In Athens, Paul's preaching was resisted by the Epicureans and Stoics (*Acts 17:18*).

The Epicureans denied the providence of God in the government of the world, the existence of the souls of men after this life and eternal rewards and punishments.

The Stoics' fundamental belief was that a man should look for all happiness in and from himself alone and from the things which are in his own power and ability to achieve.

Paul's doctrine utterly opposed these two sects and so, because it did not agree with and uphold their presuppositions and prejudices, they rejected it. And when, much later, such philosophers did profess to accept the gospel, they corrupted it by adding their own doctrinal traditions to it.

The aim of the gospel is to bring every thought into subjection to the obedience of faith. So Paul says, 'Let no one deceive himself. If anyone among you seems to be wise in this age, let him become a fool that he may become wise' (*1 Cor. 3:18*). Unless men renounce carnal wisdom and their own presuppositions and prejudices, they will never become wise by that wisdom which is from above. They must become fools to become wise. Men find the gospel resisting the natural pride of their minds and the absolute sovereignty of their reason. So they turn away from the gospel into apostasy. Refusing to become foolish, despising to become like little children, humble and teachable, they reject the gospel and follow teachers who are more suited to their proud reasonings. When corrupt man exalts his reason to absolute supremacy in religion, it is unavoidable, but each must judge that his own reason is the only standard of judgment he will accept.

So we see that in the gospel there are things which are above finite and limited reason and there are things contrary to corrupt and depraved reason.

Doctrines which are above finite, limited reason

The Trinity, the incarnation of the Son of God and the

indwelling of the Holy Spirit in all believers are above reason and so are rejected by finite, limited reason.

Doctrines which are repugnant to corrupted reason

The attributes of God, his eternal decrees, the offices and mediatorial work of Christ, justification by the imputation of Christ's righteousness, the inward regenerating and sanctifying work of the Holy Spirit and the resurrection of the dead are all repugnant to corrupt, depraved reason and so are rejected as false.

But still retaining the terms, corrupt reason puts absurd interpretations on them, interpretations which are destructive of the faith. So depraved reason seeks to bring every divine revelation into captivity to the bondage of their own perverse opinions and ideas.

This apostasy arises from the refusal to admit evangelical truths on divine authority alone.

Today there are many in the church who subject Scripture to man's finite, limited and corrupted reason. It is man's reason and not God's infallible revelation that determines what is true and what is false, what is good and what is evil. This has been so ever since this principle was first taught to man in the garden of Eden. The poison of these principles is greatly diffused in the world and the gospel is greatly corrupted. Such doctrines as eternal predestination, the total depravity of man concerning spiritual things, the power of Christ's grace in the conversion of sinners, regeneration, union with Christ, the imputation of Christ's righteousness for justification, the need for internal evangelical holiness, the need for the grace and help of the Spirit and the divine authority of the Scriptures are all rejected. Reason can see no logic in these things.

Reason exalts itself, refusing to bow to the authority of divine revelation, but determines for itself what is truth and what is goodness. Thus foolish man is led into apostasy.

Only the humble subjection of mind and conscience to the authority of God's Word will keep one safe from apostasy.

FALSE ASSURANCE AND GROUNDLESS SELF-CONFIDENCE
Neglect of the Spirit's warnings about the danger of falling into apostasy leads to a false sense of security. Therefore Christians fail to 'watch', 'to stand fast in the faith', 'to be strong and quit themselves like men' (*Matt. 24:11, 24; Rev. 3:10*). Those taken in apostasy will be utterly and eternally destroyed.

Neglect of the Spirit's warnings that, in time of great apostasy, Christians will be sleeping in false security leads to a false sense of security. They will be saying, 'Peace and safety!' when sudden destruction will come upon them (*1 Thess. 5:3*).

Love of the world, prosperity and ease, along with the cares and anxieties of life, cause many Christians to neglect these warnings and so they are in danger of falling away in times of great apostasy.

Men hear of this evil and the danger of it, but like Gallio, 'they care for none of these things'. They do not prepare themselves to contend for the faith in times of apostasy. It is this neglect that has been the cause of true religion being corrupted.

A wicked indifference and unconcern for the defence of the gospel leads many into apostasy. 'All religions are the same.' 'We all worship the same God.' 'What is truth? Who is able to say what truth is and what error is?'

Those who stand up for the gospel in such times are persecuted. Christians need to be warned (*Gal. 5:2–6; 2 Thess. 3:12; 2 Pet. 2:1, 2*).

False security leads to foolish self-confidence
Peter was foolishly self-confident that he would not deny Christ, even though all the others might do so. Christians are foolishly self-confident that they will not fall away, so they neglect the means God has given to keep them safe.

They see no need of the power of God, the intercession of Christ, the grace of the Holy Spirit to keep them from falling into apostasy. They see no need of watching and praying lest they fall into temptation.

Such foolish self-confidence soon hurries many into apostasy.

LOVE OF THE WORLD AND ITS PASSING PLEASURES IS ANOTHER CAUSE OF APOSTASY

Paul complained that Demas had forsaken him, having loved this present world (*2 Tim. 4:10*). Demas forsook the apostle and the ministry and possibly the Christian faith as well.

'The seed that fell among thorns was choked and did not yield a good crop' (*Mark 4:7, 18, 19*).

This love of the world is brought to light in times of persecution (*Matt. 13:20, 21*). When secular interests, wealth, houses, lands and possessions are endangered, then many fall away from Christ.

This love of the world is also brought to light when superstitions and error are enthroned. When worldly honour, wealth and jobs are denied to all who stand for the truth, then many succumb to apostasy.

While the warmth of the sun causes many to cast off the garment of truth, the blustering icy winds drive men to wrap the garment more tightly about them. Many Christians succumb to apostasy in times of popularity and acceptance, who would never cast off Christ in times of the severest persecutions.

Whilst the world is enthroned in men's hearts, honours and favours have more attraction than to suffer with the people of God.

SATAN ALSO DRAWS MANY INTO APOSTASY

Satan was the cause of the first apostasy from God. He himself was the first apostate. Now he is the head of all the multitudes of fallen angels 'reserved in everlasting chains under darkness for the judgment of the great day' (*Jude 6*).

Satan's great aim is to prevent people receiving the gospel, and if they do receive it, to turn them away from it.

He stirred up raging, bloody persecutions to deter people from becoming Christians. By blinding the eyes of men and filling them with prejudices against the truth, he succeeded in leading thousands away from Christ (*2 Cor. 4:4*).

Satan's aim is to corrupt men's minds (*2 Cor. 11:3*). The way he did this was by bringing in a false gospel (*v. 4*). So he raised up false teachers to be his emissaries (*vv. 14, 15*). As he deceived Eve by his false interpretation of God's Word, so he deceives many today by his false interpretations of the gospel.

God gives us many wonderful promises in his covenant of grace. These Satan attempts to pervert, opposing God's wisdom and grace in them. In this way, he hopes to draw men away from the simplicity that is in Christ and the plain declaration of God's will in the gospel to false and foolish ideas of his own. What a great part he played in the great apostasy (*2 Thess. 2:9–11*)! Satan was at work in it, bringing in strong delusions, leading many to believe his lies. So men departed from the faith, giving heed to seducing spirits (*1 Tim. 4:1*). People listen to the devil and his agents rather than to God and his ministers.

Satan is ever at work attempting to lead Christians into apostasy. He blinds their minds, inflames their lusts, pours out his temptations, involves them in false and corrupt reasonings, transforms himself into an angel of light, and uses signs and lying wonders, all to support his delusions. Satan never tires; he never goes on holiday.

GOD IS NOT AN UNCONCERNED SPECTATOR

God does not sit by and do nothing. He is 'not tempted with evil, and neither does he tempt anyone into sin or error'. But he rules all and overrules all events to his own glory.

He will not allow men to undervalue and despise, and then to reject and forsake, the greatest of his mercies, his Word and his truth, without bringing wicked apostates into the severest of judgments. So when men wickedly apostatize from his truth, God in his holy and righteous judgment gives them up to further delusions, so that they enter into full and final apostasy and grow hardened in it to their eternal destruction.

Every Christian and every Christian church needs to take heed of 2 Chronicles 15:2. God judicially forsakes those by whom he is wilfully forsaken.

The way God punishes and avenges wilful apostasy from the gospel is by delivering men wholly up to it and by hardening them in it to their eternal destruction.

He does this by first removing his lampstand from among them (*Rev. 2:5*). Christ warned backsliding Ephesus that if they did not repent, he would come and remove their lampstand from them. God will deprive apostates of the light and means of knowing the truth, so that darkness and ignorance overtakes them.

Then God sends strong delusions that they might believe a lie, because they did not love the truth (*2 Thess. 2:11*). He gives them up irrecoverably to faith in lies.

Sending a strong delusion involves three things:

(1) Firstly, God delivers up wilful apostates to the power of Satan. He does not limit Satan but allows him to lead them into the greatest delusions he can devise. This was the state of things under the papal apostasy into which Satan had succeeded in leading the greater part of the church. And to show his success, he did, as it were, have fun with the deluded

souls of men. There was nothing so foolish and stupid that he did not impose on their infantile credulity.

(2) Secondly, God delivers up wilful apostates to false teachers and deceivers. These, deceived and taught by Satan, are used by God to carry out his just displeasure on wicked apostates, whom he delivers into their power. The deceived people exalt these false teachers and deceivers into high positions in the church and then submit implicitly to them. Being in the 'temple of God', they come to the people in the place of God, claiming to speak the very words of God. With such power given to them in the church, they hold sway over the consciences of men, holding them in fear by the very positions of authority that they have been given and which they have claimed for themselves.

(3) Thirdly, God delivers up wilful apostates to blindness of mind and hardness of heart (*Isa. 6:10; John 12:39–41; Acts 28:25–27*; expounded in *Rom. 11:7, 8*).

Under these judgments – Satan, false teachers, blindness of mind and hardness of heart – the state of apostates is miserable and irrecoverable.

Let us, then, beware lest we neglect the Spirit's warnings.

7: *Apostasy from the Doctrines of the Gospel*

Many who have received the great doctrines of the gospel later turn from them and say they found nothing in them. So to prevent the same thing happening to us, we must consider why these people found nothing to satisfy them in the gospel and so have turned their backs on its great doctrines of grace.

IGNORANCE OF THEIR NEED OF JESUS CHRIST FOR SALVATION
The first major reason why many fall away from the great doctrines of grace in the gospel is because they are ignorant of their need of Jesus Christ and his grace for life and salvation. This has caused them to lose interest in him.

Such people have never experienced a deep sense of their personal need of Christ as did those at Pentecost and the Philippian gaoler (*Acts 2:37; 16:30*).

If they had had a true conviction of their need of Christ and had experienced his power in meeting that need, why do they now forsake him? A person who has been truly convinced of his need of Christ for forgiveness and salvation and has, as a result, received him by faith will never forsake Christ.

To be truly convinced of our need of Christ, we must first be convinced of the nature, guilt, pollution, power and punishment of sin, for he came to save us from our sins. No-one would have bothered to look at the brazen serpent if he had not first been bitten by a snake and knew that he was in danger of death. So none will look to Christ who are not convinced that they have sinned and will most certainly perish if Christ does not save them.

Satan's work is to excuse sin and so make the practice of it more acceptable. His aim is to make it seem that we have no real need of Christ and his sacrifice. Men are quick to believe that they are not under the power of original sin and that they are basically good, though not perfect. Spiritual sins against the gospel are considered nothing and laughed at. Immoralities against the law are treated lightly and easily passed over.

Today, the person and offices of Christ are not considered to be of any great importance and so are rarely preached.

Only the conviction of our desperate need of Christ to save us from the guilt, power, pollution and punishment of sin will drive us to Christ and keep us from turning away from him.

To be truly convinced of our need of Christ, we must first be convinced that our very best righteousnesses are utterly insufficient to enable us to stand before God in that judgment day. The solemn realization of our utter inability to do anything good and acceptable to God without Christ, and the utter insufficiency of our best deeds to stand the trial of God's judgment, will make us always aware of our need of Christ and his righteousness.

Consider that in every duty we do, how far short we fall from the standard of holiness required and how our best righteousnesses are like filthy rags! (*Isa. 64:6*).

Lack of a due sense of the sinfulness of our best works leads to dreams of self-perfection, self-righteousness and self-justification. Such dreams lead to contempt of Christ and his righteousness. Who would look for another righteousness when he is convinced that he can justify himself before God by his own righteousness?

Before people will come to Christ and stay with Christ, they need to know that they are lost, condemned sinners, standing accursed in God's sight. They need to see that Christ alone has made perfect satisfaction for the pardon of their sins and so their deliverance from eternal punishment.

People also need to know that without Christ they have no righteousness with which to stand before God and that only Christ can clothe them with that perfect righteousness which is acceptable to God, having met all the demands of his holy law.

This is the faith of God's elect against which all the works and deceits of Satan cannot prevail. The marriage of divine revelation with true experience is invincible. But those who have never seen their desperate need of Christ for these things will never persevere in believing in him, nor remain in him by faith in times of persecution and strong temptations.

LACK OF A SPIRITUAL SIGHT OF THE GLORY OF CHRIST IN HIS PERSON AND OFFICES

Under the Old Testament, Christ was revealed in the symbols and ceremonies of Old Testament worship and in God's promises. These things were the life of the faith of Old Testament saints. Abraham saw Christ's day and rejoiced (*John 8:6*). These things were diligently studied and looked into, as were all God's promises given in the prophecies (*1 Pet. 1:11; Matt. 13:17*). Their hope was to see the King Messiah in all his glory (*Isa. 33:17*). The glory and life of all Old Testament religion, of all fellowship with God, lay in these symbols, sacrifices and services, along with the promises given in prophecies. And all of them rested on that first promise given to Adam and Eve in the garden of Eden.

Christ was 'all in all' to them, as he is to us. Take Christ and his offices out of the Old Testament ministry and they become of no value or significance.

The reason the Jews rejected Christ when he came was because they could 'see neither form nor beauty in him why he should be desired' (*John 1:11; Isa. 53:2*).

So none will remain constantly faithful to Christ who is not able to spiritually discern the glory of his person and his offices.

The foundation of the apostolic faith was a personal, spiritual sight of his glory, the glory of the only-begotten Son of God (*John 1:14*). And that which they had personally experienced they endeavoured to share with others, that they also might believe and so have fellowship with him (*1 John 1:3*). This is the rock foundation of the church (*Matt. 16:16–18*). And whoever does not build on this rock builds on sand and so will not stand when the storm comes. So those who do not know Christ personally as their head will be deceived and foolishly puffed up by their fleshly minds, falling into many foolish errors (*Col. 2:18, 19*). The whole foundation of all gospel faith rests in the glory of Christ's person and offices (*Heb. 1:2, 3; Col. 1:15–19*). It is this knowledge of him alone that will make us despise all other things in comparison with him (*Phil. 3:8–10*).

So only a spiritual view of Christ's glory will preserve us from falling away from the doctrines of grace in the gospel. Satan's wicked work is to allow the full doctrine of Christ's person, but to make it seem that he is of little or no use when it comes to our salvation. This is to fight against the King of Israel.

LACK OF A PERSONAL EXPERIENCE OF THE POWER OF THE SPIRIT
AND OF THE GRACE OF CHRIST FOR THE MORTIFICATION OF SIN

Spiritual wisdom and faith are needed to seek for the help of the Spirit and the grace of Christ to mortify sin by virtue of his death. Unenlightened reason can neither see nor understand anything of this matter. In fact, this and all other mysteries of the gospel are foolish to it.

Mortification of sin is a Christian duty against which corrupted nature is opposed. 'If we by the Spirit mortify the deeds of the flesh, we shall live' – but not otherwise.

When men are aware of the great power of sin within them, they will either yield themselves up as 'servants of sin' and make 'provision for the flesh to fulfil its lusts' or will try some way or other to mortify and restrain sin within them.

Many begin by trusting in the help and strength of the Holy Spirit, but end by trusting in themselves and their own self-effort. So, no longer striving against sin by the help and strength of the Spirit, they find sin too powerful for them and so they end up by yielding themselves to the service of sin.

Why do so many in the Roman Catholic Church submit to penances, severe disciplines and self-lacerations? They do so because they are ignorant of the true and only way of mortifying sin. That true and only way is by the Spirit of Christ dwelling in true believers.

Those ignorant of God's way of mortifying sin are in danger of not doing it at all, and so ending up being servants of sin.

IGNORANCE OF THE RIGHTEOUSNESS OF GOD

It was because they were ignorant of the righteousness of God that the Jews went about trying to establish their own righteousness (*Rom. 10:3*). The Jews sought to make themselves righteous by obedience to the law (*Rom. 9:31, 32*). They thought that they were the ones who knew most about the righteousness of God because they were teachers of the law (*Rom. 2:17–20*).

The righteousness of God can mean three things. It can mean the righteousness of God himself, or it can mean that righteousness which God's law requires, or it can mean that righteousness which God has provided for the justification of sinners. It is this last righteousness that is preached in the gospel.

But before we can come to a true appreciation of that righteousness which God has provided for us for our justification, we must have a true understanding of the righteousness of God himself and that righteousness which his law requires.

The righteousness of God himself

A right understanding of the infinite purity and glorious

holiness of God's whole nature, and of his absolute eternal righteousness as the Lord and Judge of all, will teach us what ideas we ought to have of ourselves and of our need of a perfect righteousness with which to stand before him (*Heb. 12:29; Exod. 34:7; Rom. 1:32; Josh. 24:19*).

When men see the righteousness of God's character and hold him in awe and terror, they will not easily trust in their own righteousness.

Scripture shows two sorts of person who understand and grasp the righteousness of God's character. These are, firstly, convinced, guilty sinners and, secondly, humble, holy believers.

The following examples show what guilty convinced sinners think of themselves and their own righteousness: Adam (*Gen. 3:10*); others (*Isa. 33:14; Mic. 6:6, 7*). Either they think of fleeing and hiding from God, or they attempt impossible ways of atoning for their sins, or they are swallowed up in despair.

Send them in this state to their own righteousness and they will think that you are mocking them by increasing their sense of misery and horrible despair.

Holy, humble believers all acknowledge that such is the holiness and righteousness of God that none can stand before him in his own righteousness (*Job 4:17, 19; 9:2; Psa. 130:3; 143:2*).

It is the lack of due meditation on this truth that has led to many presumptuous ideas in the world concerning the justification of sinners.

Scripture, speaking of justification, teaches us not to try and understand it until we have seen ourselves as God sees us (*Psa. 143:2; Rom. 3:20*). Then we can consider on what ground we may stand before him.

But men, ignorant of God's righteous character, think God is like themselves, that is, one who is either not so holy in himself, or one who does not require such a high standard of holiness from us. They see God as one who is not concerned about our duties and much less about our sins. Is it any wonder, then, that men think they can stand before him in their own righteousness?

Some teach that there is no such severity in God against sin, and no such holiness in him to arouse him to wrath against sin.

So all ideas of a self-righteousness or justification by works have always produced lives of a low moral standard.

When righteousness by works was enthroned in the papacy before the Reformation, the lives of the people were particularly brutal and cruel in their wickedness, and most of their good works were but barterings with God and conscience for the forgiveness of horrible vices and immoralities.

Justification by works was supposed to produce holiness and righteousness among men, but it only succeeded in producing unholy, unrighteous lives. The reason was because the same ideas of God which allowed men to suppose they may be justified in his sight by their own good works allowed them also to fulfil their lusts, because they believed that God would not be so unloving as to treat their sins with great severity.

Self-righteousness and loose living have always gone together. Only grace and justification by faith alone in the imputed righteousness of Christ will put a stop to sin.

He that drives men into self-righteousness at one door opens another for their sins.

The righteousness which the law of God requires from us

Were people acquainted with the purity, spirituality, severity and relentlessness of the law, they would not dream that their own self-righteousness can ever meet its demands.

But when men think that the law is only concerned with the outward behaviour and only with great sins, then they easily excuse themselves with many pharisaical distinctions and expositions of the law. When we do not realize that the true purpose of the law is to examine us to see if we come up to the standard of God's image in our heart, soul, mind and outward behaviour, that image in which we were created, and that it will punish the least deviation from that image, then we may be satisfied with our own self-righteousness.

The righteousness which God has provided for us in the gospel (*Rom. 10:3, 4*)

This is 'the righteousness which is of faith' (*Rom. 9:30*). The righteousness of God is that righteousness which Christ has wrought for us by his life of perfect obedience to the law, along with the perfect satisfaction he made to the demands of holy infinite justice by his sufferings and death on the cross. Those who are ignorant of this righteousness will go about establishing their own righteousness and trusting to it alone.

But when a person is convicted of sin, his mouth is stopped and he stands guilty before God. Then the gospel of God's righteousness is preached to him (*Rom. 3:21–26*; with *Rom. 5: 18, 19*).

He who has truly trusted in Christ as the One who has, on his behalf, fulfilled the whole law and freed him from all its demands for justification before God will not hold Christ's righteousness imputed to him in contempt or treat it with scorn. When men despise, neglect or reject the righteousness which Christ has wrought for us, then they 'crucify afresh the Son of God and put him to an open shame'.

When people say they have tried Christ's righteousness and did not find anything in it, so now are trusting in their own righteousness, they do him great dishonour and bring upon themselves the full judgment and wrath of God on their wicked apostasy.

UNWILLINGNESS TO SUBMIT TO THE SOVEREIGNTY OF GOD

The sovereign, infinite wisdom and grace of God is the sole foundation of the covenant of grace in which God promises eternal salvation to all who put their faith in Jesus Christ for justification. The sovereignty of God's wisdom runs throughout the whole mystery of the gospel and is the reason for the incarnation of the Son of God and his being filled with all grace to be the Saviour of sinners (*John 3:16; Col. 1:19; John 1:16*).

God's sovereign wisdom and grace sent Christ to be our substitute, to stand surety for our sins, to be punished for them in our place (*Isa. 53:6, 10; 2 Cor. 5:21*).

Eternal election also arises from the sovereignty of God's wisdom and grace (*Rom. 9:11, 18*). So does that inward effective call of the Spirit, bringing elect sinners to repentance and faith by the preaching of the gospel (*Matt. 11:25, 26*). Justification by faith is also the effect of sovereign infinite wisdom and grace (*Rom. 3:30*). And the same may be said of all the other mysteries of the gospel. Sovereign love, grace and goodness, poured out on those God chooses to pour them out on, is put to us in the gospel as a truth to be received and believed.

But the carnal, unspiritual, unconverted mind is not pleased with any of this, but rises up in opposition to it. It cannot tolerate the idea that the will, wisdom and pleasure of God is to be submitted to and adored, even if it cannot be understood. So the incarnation and the cross of Christ, the Son of God, are foolishness to it (*1 Cor. 1:23–25*). The decrees of God concerning election and reprobation are considered unfair, unjust and subversive of all religion (*Rom. 9:17–21*). It considers that justification through the imputation of the righteousness of Christ perverts the law and makes all our righteousness unnecessary. In the same way, the carnal mind rises up in opposition to the whole mystery of the gospel, all its doctrines, commands and promises as arising from the sovereignty of God. It resists that faith which lies in giving glory to God by believing the things that are above man's finite, limited reason and which is repulsive to corrupt, selfish reason (*Rom. 11:18–21*).

So, in opposition to God's sovereign will and wisdom, men set up their inner light as the standard by which gospel truths must be measured. Instead of becoming fools, by submitting their reason and wisdom to the sovereignty of God, so that they might be truly wise, they have become wise in their own conceits, and so have grown proud in their foolishness.

There is no broader way to apostasy than to reject God's sovereignty in all things concerning the revelation of himself and our obedience, refusing to 'bring into captivity every thought to the obedience of Christ'. From the refusal to submit to God's sovereignty over all things, including our eternal salvation, arose Pelagianism, Arminianism and every present-day heresy.

LACK OF EVIDENCE IN THEMSELVES OF THE DIVINE AUTHORITY OF THE SCRIPTURES

He that has not experienced for himself the divine evidences which God has put into Scripture as proofs of their divine origin will not stand firm when persecution and trouble arise. God looks with respect to those alone who tremble at his word and recognize his authority in it. But where the personal experience of God's authority in Scripture is lacking, the 'unlearned and unstable' are bold to 'wrest the Scriptures to their own destruction' or to prefer other things, such as tradition and reason, to them, or at least to be equal in authority with them.

It is not enough, therefore, that we assent to the truth of the Word of God, unless we have also experienced its power, have submitted to its claims made in God's name, and have subjected absolutely our souls and consciences to it. Against this, every imagination of the carnal mind exalts itself to claim equal right and authority with God's holy Word. The result of all this is that God gives men up to 'strong delusions that they may believe a lie' because they did not 'receive' or retain the 'love of the truth' (*2 Thess. 2:10, 11*). And when it comes to this, Satan leads them into endless delusions, making them obstinate and stubborn in their heresies.

This is the first way in which men fall away from the gospel. They find nothing beneficial to themselves in its doctrines, and so by rejecting that which was devised by the infinite wisdom of God and wrought for us by his glorious Son, they do their best to 'crucify him afresh and so put him to open shame'.

8: *Apostasy from the Commands of the Gospel*

Apostasy from the holy commands of the gospel is, in many ways, more dreadful and dangerous than a partial apostasy from its truth. Under such apostasy it is easy to be greatly hardened by the deceitfulness of sin into thinking that there is not much evil and danger in it. Error in the doctrine of the gospel is soon noticed and men are warned of it. But when the whole world is drowned in lusts and pleasures, let the lives of men be as contrary to the rule of the gospel as darkness is to light, as long as they do not disturb outward worship and continue to be good Catholics or good Protestants, nothing will be said to warn them.

It is generally acknowledged that it is possible that men may please God and be accepted with him, notwithstanding many misunderstandings and mistakes concerning the doctrine of the gospel. But that any should come to enjoy God who lives and dies unrepentant of any sin against the holy commands of the gospel is not taught by any. For to pretend that men may live habitually sinful lives without any attempt by the Spirit to mortify sin in them, nor with any desire for repentance, is to deny the Christian religion. So apostasy from the holy commands of the gospel is at least as dangerous and as much to be opposed and resisted as that apostasy from gospel doctrines. So we ought to be more earnestly warned of it. Apostasy from the holiness of the gospel is as dishonouring to Christ as is apostasy from its doctrines. Paul warns Timothy of this apostasy (*1 Tim. 4:1*). I believe that this warning given to Timothy had its greatest fulfilment in the papacy; but it does not refer to them alone, but to us also and to the times in which we live.

Paul also warns that in these 'latter times', under an outward profession of the gospel, men would give themselves up to the vilest lusts and the practice of the most abominable sins (2 *Tim. 3:1–5*).

If this apostasy threatens us, we ought to stand on our guard so that we are not taken by surprise and overcome by it. We ought to 'pass the time of our sojourning here in fear'! It is no time for any to be careless and sit in false security if we are serious about being kept safe from this fatal evil. None of us, however, can say that we have not been warned to watch and to diligently seek divine help.

If we are faithfully living in obedience to the gospel, we need not be greatly moved or 'shaken in our minds' when we see these things come to pass. Our faith is based on the infallibility of Scripture. Its prophecies and predictions have foretold and warned us of these things, so that when they come to pass we know we are in those 'latter times' (*Matt. 24:9–13, 24; Acts 20:29, 30; 2 Thess. 2:3; 1 Tim. 4:1–3; 2 Tim. 3:1–5*). There is nothing more pernicious than for any Christian or for any church to think that these things will not come on them and therefore they need not be watchful, nor need they pray for divine help.

When the Jews fell into such self-confidence in their temple and their worship, God bade them remember what happened to Shiloh, where the tabernacle was first set up when they entered Canaan. He warned them that what had happened once could easily happen again. And we can see what happened to the first Christian churches and how soon they fell into apostasy (*Rev. 2:4, 5; 3:1–3, 14–17*). We may go to them and learn how foolish are all who trust in outward privileges.

The doctrine of the gospel is a doctrine which leads to holiness.

It teaches, requires and commands holiness. It teaches that 'without holiness, no one shall see the Lord'.

The holiness required by the gospel is an obedience of quite another kind and nature than that obedience required by any other doctrine or teaching.

Natural law suggests many important duties to God, to ourselves and to other men. The written law presents to us all those moral duties which God required from man when he was created. But there is a holiness required by the gospel which, though it includes all the demands of the moral law, yet it is different in the nature of the obedience required and the motives of that holy obedience. The holy obedience which the gospel requires arises from gratitude for salvation received, and not that servile obedience which arises from the search for merit.

Together with the preaching of the doctrine of the gospel, there is a work of the Spirit, which is to convince men of sin, righteousness and judgment (*Isa. 59:21; John 16:7–11*). The Lord Christ, by his Spirit, carries out this work whenever the Word of God is preached according to his mind and will. By this work on their souls, men are brought to holiness of heart and holiness of life. By the Word of God and the Spirit of Christ, multitudes have been made holy, and multitudes more are still being called out of this world to holiness of life. These shall never utterly and finally fall away from true holiness, but shall be preserved by the power of God through faith unto salvation. Yet even these may fall away from wholehearted obedience to the holy commands of the gospel and become for a while unfruitful in their lives. In every backsliding there is partial apostasy, with much dishonour done to Christ. Nor does any-one know whether his backsliding will not end in total apostasy.

It is so also with churches. When churches were first planted in the world by the apostles, they were in a pure and holy state as to the doctrine, professed holiness and worship of the gospel. They were all, when planted, noble vines of pure seed, but later they turned 'into the degenerate plant of a strange vine'. From being pure virgins betrothed to Christ, they fell into spiritual harlotry, and by their falling away, they no longer glorified Christ, nor did they reveal his power and effectiveness in the world. And the blessing which they should have brought to the nations of the world was lost and forfeited.

Where true holiness exists, and the power of it is seen by its fruits, there and there alone Christ is glorified and honoured in the world. It is true there are other things required of us by our Lord and King to bring glory to him, such as witnessing to the truth and the observance of gospel worship. But if these things are not accompanied by a holy life, they in no way advance the glory of Christ.

But where churches and persons professing the gospel are changed and renewed into the image of God; where their hearts are purified and their outward behaviour is fruitful; where they are under the control of a spirit of peace, love, meekness, kindness, self-denial and heavenly-mindedness, and they are fruitful in good works, which things are the substance of true holiness, there they truly show forth in the world the glory of the gospel and of its author. By these things, they prove the power, purity and effectiveness of his doctrine and grace, and so he is glorified. In this faithful witness, Christ sees 'the travail of his soul and is satisfied' (*Isa. 53:11*).

But where men and churches are called by his name, profess his authority, expect mercy and blessedness from him, and at the same time fall short of this holiness and walk contrary to it, then is the holy Son of God 'crucified afresh and put to an open shame'.

TWO KINDS OF APOSTASY FROM GOSPEL HOLINESS

Some reject the kind of obedience the gospel requires for another kind of obedience, another set of laws. Or else they accept gospel laws and duties, but reject gospel motives. This is one sort of apostasy from gospel holiness.

Others fall away from gospel holiness totally and give themselves up completely to sinful lives. This is that apostasy which the world groans under today, and which, it is to be feared, will bring the judgments of God upon it. The true profession of Christianity is lost and held in contempt by many. Holy duties, disciplined behaviour, growing in grace and in the knowledge of the Lord are not only neglected, but scorned.

In many places it is useless to seek for Christianity amongst Christians.

APOSTASY OF THE CHURCH OF ROME

Romanists are the supreme example of those who have turned away from the holy ways of gospel obedience into paths which they have made for themselves

None boast more of holiness than does the Roman Catholic Church. They claim their church is the true church because of its sanctity. But because of the unholy lives of the majority of Roman Catholics, and also of many of their chief rulers and guides, they point to those who have taken vows of poverty, chastity and obedience, and who have dedicated themselves to a monastic life and to stricter rules and duties than others reach up to, or are obliged to submit to. These alone have obtained the name of *religious* among them. But many have already discovered the vanity, superstition and hypocrisy of their daily routines in which they generally spend their time. But this holy obedience is not that required and commanded in the gospel.

Romish vows of holiness do not show the spiritual freedom of gospel holiness

The first thing that truth does in our minds is to free them from all error and prejudices (*John 8:32*). Truth is the principle of all holiness, enlarging the mind and spirit. So it is called 'true holiness' or 'the holiness of truth' (*Eph. 4:24*). So 'where the Spirit of the Lord (or the Spirit of truth) is, there is liberty' (*2 Cor. 3:17*).

Men are, since the fall, 'servants of sin', willingly giving themselves up to its service, satisfying its lusts and obeying its commands. In such a state, they are 'free from righteousness'. They refuse to serve and obey the demands of righteousness. But where the Holy Spirit works with the Word of truth, men are freed from sin and become servants to God, producing holy fruit in their lives (*Rom. 6:20, 22*). So it is said of all believers that they 'have not received the spirit of bondage again to fear, but have received the Spirit of adoption by whom we cry Abba, Father' (*Rom. 8:15*). They have not received the 'spirit of fear, but of power, and of love and of a sound mind' (*2 Tim. 1:7*).

The teaching of the whole of Scripture is that the hearts of believers, by God's grace, are freed from fear of judgment, to a free, willing, cheerful spirit that loves to do all the duties that holiness requires, moved by gratitude for mercies received. They are not driven by fear to a scrupulous bondage to outward duties, but with delight and true freedom of will they gladly obey. Because they have received the 'Spirit of adoption', they live as children of God, honouring their Father by doing his will gladly and out of gratitude for the great salvation which he has wrought for us in and through Christ.

But there are strong proofs that those who place themselves under Romish vows and strict monastic rules of life and who spend their days in many outward religious duties, which the Church of Rome calls holiness, are not free, but are ruled by a servile, slavish spirit. They are forced to bind themselves and to be bound by their vows if they wish to live in that community, which is contrary to all true Christian fellowship. In obeying these vows, they are not their own masters, free to discipline and rule themselves, but are under the strict discipline of others who administer outward punishments in cases of failure. *Those who are servants of men in religious duties are not God's freemen*, nor do they have Christ for their Lord who subject themselves religiously to men.

What drives these men to a monastic life, and to strict religious rules of life invented by men, are vows and rules of life nowhere required by God or our Lord Christ in the gospel. And the chief reason why they continue in this life is the obedience which they have vowed and so owe to their superiors.

It is easy to see how opposite this way is to true spiritual freedom of mind which is the root of all true gospel holiness. Romish vows and rules of religious life are also motivated by thoughts of achieving merit, which stimulates them to further religious disciplines. The desire to achieve merit also makes for a servile, slavish spirit in all that they do, for they cannot but know that everything done in order to achieve merit must not only be tried by the strict, relentless standard of perfect sincerity, but also weighed in the balance of absolute perfection. This thought utterly destroys that free, willing, cheerful, glad obedience given out of gratitude for the free gift of justification and eternal life. Those under Romish vows are also driven to obedience by the tormenting thought *that they have no assurance either that they are accepted by God in this life, or ever shall be accepted by him in the next*. So in all their duties, they are of necessity driven by a 'spirit of fear' and not 'of power and of a sound mind'.

Romish vows and rules of religious life bind men to observe that which is not commanded by the gospel, but is a system of laws and rules invented by men.

[107]

So some obey the rule of Benedict, some of Francis, some of Dominic, some of Ignatius and the like. This proves that all that they do has nothing to do with gospel holiness, for that holiness is conformity to the rule of the gospel, which is the will of God. Thus, like the Pharisees of old whom Christ rebuked, they add duties not commanded by God. So, 'in vain they worship God, teaching for doctrines the commands of men' (*Matt. 15:6, 9*). Let the number of false, invented duties of religion be ever so great, let the manner of their performance be ever so exact or severe, they only divert the minds of men from the obedience which the gospel requires. 'As plants which the heavenly Father never planted, they shall, in due time, be rooted up' and cast into the fire (*Matt. 15:13*).

There is nothing in all that is prescribed by the masters of these rules and vows, or practised by their disciples, but it may all be done without either faith in Christ or a sense of his love to souls.

On the other hand, the obedience the gospel requires is the 'obedience of faith'. On that and on no other root will gospel holiness grow. And the chief nature of gospel holiness is 'the love of Christ' which alone 'constrains' to it (*2 Cor. 5:14*).

But what is there in all these monastic vows and rules of life that makes it necessary for them to be carried out for the love of Christ? May not men rise at midnight to repeat a number of prayers, or go barefoot, or wear sackcloth, or abstain from meat on occasions or always, or submit to discipline from themselves or others and, if strong enough, undergo all the horrid and indeed ridiculous hardships without the least dram of saving faith or love? All false religions have always had some among them who have loved to amuse others with their self-inflicted punishments and penances.

All the good that these Romish vows and rules of life do is utterly corrupted by the proud thought of gaining merit and doing works of supererogation, works above all that was required of them, which can then be used to help others to achieve the required standard of merit. The whole idea of merit and works of supererogation utterly weakens the covenant of grace, treats with contempt the blood and mediation of Christ, and is totally inconsistent with the fundamental principles of the gospel.

And when we add to these vows all the gross superstition and idolatry to which they give themselves up in their devotions, then we can see that, notwithstanding all Rome's claims to holiness and a more strict obedience to duties than other men, yet it is clear that the best of their works falls far below the standard of the holiness required by the gospel and without which no-one shall see the Lord.

APOSTASY UNDER PRETENCE OF MORALITY

Some fall away from the commands of the gospel under the guise of morality. They deride anything which is required above what they call decent, moral behaviour as 'foolish fanaticism'.

Some claim that all the obedience that the gospel requires is a decent, moral, upright life, where each person 'does his best', but which has no need of the help of evangelical grace.

Others say that this moral behaviour falls short of that true holiness which the gospel requires. Gospel obedience is the performance of all moral duties in the power and grace of Christ to the glory of God. So whoever fails to make good use of moral virtues or moral duties is disobedient to the gospel and its laws.

But men may do what is morally good and yet never do anything that is acceptable to God, for they may not do it out of love and gratitude to God for his grace and mercy, but for the love and praise of self.

Morality becomes apostasy when it is ruled and directed by the light of conscience and not by the gospel principles described above. The light of conscience can only direct men to those moral virtues which, by the law of creation, are obligatory to all mankind. Conscience can never direct men to that spiritual obedience which the gospel requires.

Morality arising only from conviction, performed by the strength of reason alone, without the special supernatural help of the Spirit and the grace of God, is not gospel obedience. Whatever is not wrought in us by the grace of God, as well as by us, is not evangelical obedience and so is not acceptable to God.

Morality which does not come from the spiritual regeneration and renovation of our souls is not gospel holiness. The tree must first be made good and then the fruit will be good also. All morality arising from the old nature – even if prayer is made to Christ for help and it is claimed that it is being done to the glory of God – is never acceptable to God. Unless a person is regenerate and his nature renewed into the image and likeness of God; unless he is endued with spiritual life from above enabling him to live to God, he can do nothing that is acceptable to God. Any morality that does not arise from this principle of grace in the renewed soul is not gospel holiness.

Morality claimed by those who are really destitute of the internal illumination of the Spirit, enabling them to discern spiritual things in a spiritual manner and to know the mysteries of the kingdom of God, is not gospel holiness.

Morality separated from those fundamental, supernatural gospel graces born of divine truth supernaturally revealed is not true gospel holiness. Such supernatural truths in particular as the mediation of Christ and the Spirit abiding with the church as her Comforter are the truths on which true gospel morality is based. Morality divorced from the doctrines of the gospel is not that holiness which the gospel requires.

So if any turn away from true gospel morality to natural morality, they have fallen away from gospel holiness and are in danger of irrecoverable apostasy.

APOSTASY UNDER PRETENCE OF PERFECTION

Some fall away from true gospel holiness by claiming their behaviour is perfect. Such a claim is destructive of the covenant of grace, of all need for the mediation and the continual cleansing by the blood of Christ and is contrary to the numberless testimonies of Scripture and the experience of all believers (e.g., *1 John 1: 8-10*).

The above examples are some instances of apostasy from true evangelical holiness.

THE HOLINESS WHICH THE GOSPEL REQUIRES

Gospel holiness requires continual spiritual warfare if it is to be maintained. The devil, the flesh and the world will strive to drive us away from true gospel holiness to something less, but which is not acceptable to God.

So we are to '*resist*' the devil (*1 Pet. 5:8, 9*). To do this, we must take up the whole armour of God (*Eph. 6:12, 13*).

We are to '*flee*' those fleshly lusts which war against the soul (*1 Pet. 2:11*).

And we are '*not to love the world or the things in the world*' (*1 John 2:15*). But we are to overcome it by faith, that faith that believes that Jesus is the Son of God (*1 John 5:4, 5*).

God will not accept lazy, slothful performances of some duties and abstinence from some sins. Crucifying sin, mortifying unrestrained lusts, resisting the devil, fleeing fleshly lusts and not loving the world are all gospel duties to be constantly maintained whilst we live in this world.

As the Israelites were disheartened and discouraged by the ten spies when they first arrived at the borders of Canaan, so many who are not far from the kingdom of God are discouraged and disheartened when told of this lifelong spiritual warfare (*Numb. 13:32; Mark 12:34*). If they are not careful, they see the spiritual giants waiting for them, but do not see the power and grace of Christ. Only those who are truly 'born again' will enter the kingdom of God and do battle.

Some endeavour to enter the kingdom of God who are not regenerate and have no spiritual strength to contend with the enemies of holiness. They think to win through by the strength of the flesh alone.

But soon the flesh grows weary. Excuses are made for not continuing in some duties. The flesh has great support from the carnal, unspiritual, unconverted mind. One duty after another is omitted and finally forsaken. The duty of keeping the body in subjection is neglected (*1 Cor. 9:27*).

True believers will be humbled for such dereliction of duty and by the grace of God will return to their former diligence (*Psa. 119:176*). But hypocrites will not be troubled overmuch for neglecting gospel duties.

Indwelling sin will fight against holiness and will often prevail. It succeeds in wearying the mind with its continuous pleas for its old dominion. The hypocrite in time gives heed to indwelling sin, whereas the believer takes hold of the promise that 'sin shall not have dominion' over him (*Rom. 6:14*).

The unconverted person is ignorant of the true way of coming to the Lord Christ for the grace and the help of the Spirit to keep him in a state of gospel holiness. So he has to fend for himself and soon is satisfied with that holiness which the flesh can produce. But a true Christian is not satisfied with a holiness that can be produced and that can exist without Christ and his Spirit. The Christian knows that without Christ he can do nothing, much less produce a holiness acceptable to God (*John 15:5*).

As ignorance of Christ's righteousness is the reason why men go about trying to establish their own righteousness, so ignorance of how to live continually by the grace and strength of Christ is the reason why many turn to a lower standard of holiness, which is no holiness at all.

The unconverted person does not know and cannot produce a true evangelical repentance. Repentance is the gift of God (*Acts 5:31; 11:18; 2 Tim. 2:25*). It is this grace of true repentance that carries believers through all their failings, weaknesses and sins. It is the doorway to holiness and the guardian that keeps true believers in holiness. Repentance does this by keeping believers in humble self-abasement, arising from a sense of the majesty and holiness of God and a recognition of how far short of his glory are their best duties. He that is not aware of the gracious sweetness in and the great usefulness of true repentance does not know what it is to walk with God. Whoever can taste no spiritual comfort in his sorrows from this grace of repentance, who thinks that repentance has to do only with the law and the fear of judgment, will not easily live in the practice of repentance every day of his life.

Gospel holiness requires constant, habitual obedience in all duties, and forbids any one lust of the mind or of the flesh

We are to be 'perfecting holiness in the fear of God' (*2 Cor. 7:1*). No provision is to be made for the flesh to fulfil its lusts (*Rom. 13:14*). These are the terms of the gospel. Not one duty is to be neglected. Not one sin is to be indulged.

The gospel provides merciful relief and pardon for those daily sins which overcome us because of our weakness (*1 Pet. 4:1, 2*). Yet it will not allow one sin to be spared, cherished and loved. An habitual life of sin is utterly inconsistent with evangelical obedience (*1 John 3:6–9*).

The perfection required in the new covenant is sincerity, integrity, freedom from deceit and walking after the Spirit and not after the flesh, in newness of life (*Gen. 17:1; 1 John 3:7–10*).

This is why so many fall away from the gospel.

They cannot see sin as the gospel sees it, nor judge those things to be sin and evil which the gospel declares to be so. Under this darkness and ignorance, all sorts of filthy lusts are cherished in the hearts of men. They have a willing insensibility of the guilt of some unmortified lust. The rich young man who came to Christ would not take up his cross and follow Christ because the love of riches was in his heart.

The witch whom King Saul consulted had a 'familiar spirit'. At first, the devil is feared, but then as he is daily entertained, he becomes a familiar spirit. The deceived person thinks the devil is in his power when in reality he is in the devil's power. It is the same with any unmortified lust. It becomes a familiar lust. Man thinks he is in control of that lust and can cast it out when he pleases. But in reality the lust is in control of him.

Such people are willingly ignorant of the inward, spiritual extent of the commands of the gospel. A generous mind, freed from superstitious fears by education, will deliver man from all his feelings of guilt. So the educated person comes to believe that guilt over small sins promotes only the interests of preachers. Few can understand the filth and pollution of sin.

'Why should we trouble ourselves over trivial, minor faults?' they ask. How easily people are deceived by their corruptions when they have no sense of the holiness of God and the holiness of his law.

Pride, ambition, covetousness, love of the world, uncleanness, greediness, boasting and idleness all call for the indulgence of one sin or another.

Such persons are not approved of by God and have no ground to expect his blessing or help. One sin makes a man guilty of the whole law (*James 2:10*). The psalmist said that if he regarded iniquity in his heart, the Lord would not hear him (*Psa. 66:18*).

The indulgence of one sin opens the door to further sins.

The indulgence of one sin diverts the soul from the use of those means by which all other sins should be resisted.

People also turn away from gospel holiness because its graces are not thought highly of in the world

Moral philosophers proclaimed their love of virtue because it went hand in hand with their own honour, glory and reputation. Those virtues they considered to be the greatest were the ones seen and praised by men. The Pharisees did their religion to be seen by men. Self-love and the love of men's praise was the motive of all their religion.

But meekness, gentleness, self-denial, poverty of spirit, mourning for sin, hungering and thirsting after righteousness, mercy and compassion, purity of heart, honesty and simplicity of spirit, readiness to undergo and to forgive injuries, zeal for God, contempt for the world and fear of sinning and of God's judgments on sin are not praised by men.

But these are the precious jewels of the heart with which God is pleased.

The world, however, thinks they are weak, superstitious, silly and senseless. The world does not realize that gospel holiness deals with the heart and mind, which no mortal eye can see and with which few are concerned. So gospel virtues are rejected in favour of those virtues which the world holds in high esteem.

When the great apostasy began and the churches turned from the power and purity of the gospel, the first thing was to get people to neglect the chief graces of the gospel, such as the need for regeneration and a heavenly principle of spiritual life, by encouraging splendid works of piety and

[115]

charity. It did not matter that their minds were defiled, their lusts unmortified, their hearts proud and stubborn, and their souls destitute of spiritual and heavenly graces, for these outward glorious works, seen and praised by men, would assuredly bring them to a blessed immortality in eternal glory.

This hypocritical veil being torn apart, let us beware lest we neglect outward duties which are to the glory of God and the good of mankind for inward graces alone. True gospel holiness not only purifies the inward man, but also leads to those good works 'which God prepared beforehand that we should walk in them' (*Eph. 2:10*).

9: *Apostasy and the Ordained Ministry*

The purity or apostasy of a church greatly depends on its ministers, leaders, teachers and preachers, just as the church in the Old Testament depended for its purity on the faithfulness of its priests (*Mal. 2:1–9*).

The holy, humble, hardworking ministry which Christ instituted in the church was greatly used in converting men to, and keeping them in, evangelical obedience. Their doctrine, spirit, example, lives, prayers, preaching and hard work were blessed and prospered by God. The lives of these Christians backed up and proved the power and truth of the gospel they preached.

But through the degeneracy of the following ages, the streams of Christian religion were polluted by corrupt teachers who were sad examples of strife, divisions, ambitions and worldly-mindedness.

Under the Old Testament, the priests led the people into two different kinds of apostasy:

First, they led the people into superstition and idolatry (*Jer. 23:9–15*). This apostasy ended in the Babylonian captivity, where all their idols were buried in the land of Shinar (*Zech. 5:11*).

Secondly, after their return from captivity, the priests, by negligence, ignorance and evil example, led the people into contempt for God and sacred things. This began in the days of the prophet Malachi, the last of the biblical prophets, and ended in the rejection of Christ and the destruction of that church and nation. When Christ was rejected by the people, it was the religious leaders who forced them to cry out, 'Crucify him!'

Similarly, the first apostasy in the Christian church was by superstition and idolatry, which came to its height in the Church of Rome. This superstition and idolatry was inevitably accompanied by increased wickedness in the lives of all sorts of people.

Many churches, delivered from superstition and idolatry, fell into worldly, sensual, profane behaviour, because the ministry in those churches was worldly, sensual and profane.

How important, then, is the appointed ministry in keeping the church pure and preventing it from falling into apostasy.

The purity and well-being of a church depends on the purity and faithfulness of its ministers (Eph. 4:11–15).

The church thrives or falls into decay as its appointed ministry thrives or decays. If ministers are negligent and corrupt, the people will fall away from the gospel. The flocks will not be preserved where the shepherds are negligent. Fields will be overrun with weeds, thorns and briers if they are not continually cared for.

IMPORTANT DUTIES OF THE MINISTRY

It is the duty of the appointed ministry to keep pure the doctrine of the gospel, especially that concerning holiness. 'The priest's lips are to keep knowledge' (*Mal. 2:7; Eph. 4:11–15*). This was the chief charge Paul gave to the elders at Ephesus (*Acts 20:28–30*). Paul also charges Timothy to keep the gospel pure (*1 Tim. 6:13, 14, 20; 2 Tim. 2:14, 15*). And this doctrine of the gospel is to be committed to faithful men who will be able to teach others also (*2 Tim. 2:1, 2*).

Scripture, the minds and hearts of believers, and the appointed and ordained ministry are the three repositories of sacred truth.

[118]

Scripture is kept safe by God's providence against all oppositions of hell and the world.

Sacred truth in the minds and hearts of believers is kept by the Spirit of Christ and his grace (*John 14:16, 17, 26; 16:13; I John 2:20, 21; John 6:45; Heb. 8:10, 11*). It is the work of the Holy Spirit to preserve the truth in the hearts and minds of believers, even in the times of the Romish apostasy, as he did in the days of Israel's apostasy, when Elijah seemed to stand alone for true religion. Then God had kept seven thousand who did not bow the knee to Baal (*I Kings 19:18*).

All the preaching and teaching of sacred truth is committed to the appointed ministry. The imagination of the Church of Rome that sacred truth is kept in the hidden cells of tradition or in invisible, fantastic treasuries which require neither care, nor wisdom, nor honesty in keeping it pure, but only a pretence of keys to open it, was one way by which truth and holiness were driven out of the world.

Gospel truth is the only root from which gospel holiness grows. If the root is corrupt, the fruit will be corrupt also. It is impossible to maintain the power of godliness where the doctrine from which it comes is unknown, corrupted or despised. On the other hand, where men are tired of holiness, they will not long continue faithful to divine truth. The great opposition made to every gospel doctrine today is because men dislike holiness.

It is the duty of ministers to teach the whole counsel of God. Any who are not endowed with wisdom to see what is useful, profitable, and what their hearers are ready for, according to the present need of their spiritual state, do not know what it is to be faithful ministers of Christ.

It is the duty of the appointed ministry to preach the whole counsel of God, as did Paul (*Acts 20:27*).

They must preach the whole counsel of God with care, diligence and faithfulness (*2 Tim. 4:1, 2*). How these words to Timothy ought to ring in the ears of all ministers who wish to carry out their duty faithfully. Will the souls of men be preserved, edified and saved with less effort than in the days of the apostles?

They must preach the whole counsel of God with all their strength (*Acts 6:4; 1 Tim. 5:17; 1 Cor. 16:16; 1 Thess. 5:12*).

They must preach the whole counsel of God with constant prayer (*Acts 6:4*). That ministry of the Word not backed by prayer for its success is not likely to have any blessing on it. Paul is the supreme example of a man of prayer (*Rom. 1:9, 10*). It is useless to take up the whole armour of God if we do not back it up with prayer (*Eph. 6:18, 19*). A minister who preaches the Word of God without constant prayer for its success is likely to be harbouring secret atheism in his heart and very unlikely to work holiness in the lives of others.

It is the duty of the appointed ministry to represent, by their lives and by their ministry, the power and truth of the great and holy doctrines which they preach.

It is the duty of the appointed ministers to show forth in their lives, meekness, humility and zeal for God. They are to show moderation, self-denial and readiness for the cross. They are above all called to mortify, by the Spirit, their corrupt desires. Contempt for the world, kindness and patience to all men, and heavenly-mindedness should all be marks of a minister of Christ and the gospel.

Whatever vices and corruptions men see in the lives of their ministers will not be attributed to the depravity of their old nature which still abides in them, but to the gospel. So, in all things, ministers must show themselves a pattern of good works (*Titus 2:7*). They must be examples to all who follow them (*2 Thess. 3:9; 1 Tim. 4:12*). This is the honour to which Christ calls his ministers.

It is the duty of the appointed ministry to attend diligently to that rule and holy discipline which the Lord Christ has appointed for the edification of the church and the preservation of its purity, holiness and obedience.

Many ministers are woefully ignorant of the counsel of God. They have not been faithful in keeping the truth, doctrine and mysteries of the gospel pure and uncorrupt. They have no desire or ability to search into the mysteries of the doctrine of Christ. They despise the hard work of faithfully expounding the Scriptures. So multitudes perish through lack of knowledge. They must and will die in their sins, but their blood will be required at the hand of such faithless ministers (*Ezek. 3:16–21*).

How brutishly ignorant are the majority of priests in the papacy. But it does not matter to them, for their work is to keep the people ignorant of the doctrines of Scripture. Neither is it any better in the Greek Orthodox Church. As a result, whole nations calling themselves Christians have, through stupid ignorance, degenerated into disrespect and contempt for holy things and tolerate abominable immoralities worse than any tolerated by heathens.

If the preaching of the gospel is the only sovereign, effectual means appointed by God for the regeneration and renovation of men's natures and the reformation of their lives (to deny which would be to deny Christianity itself), it is vain to expect that either of them will be wrought in such a way as to restore the beauty and glory of religion in the world, unless an able ministry is provided to teach the people.

But through a faithless, corrupt ministry, such as is to be found in the Church of Rome, the truth has been debased, corrupted and perverted. Neither is there, in our day, any one doctrine that should promote evangelical obedience which is free from being despised or corrupted.

For the truth to be kept pure, prayer must be made to God. Only by his grace will the ministry be enabled to keep the Word of God free from corruption.

Many ministers are lazy, cold and indifferent to their work. Few diligently and industriously give themselves wholeheartedly to the utmost of their strength and ability to the work of the ministry, with zeal for the glory of God and with heartfelt compassion for the souls of men.

Can anyone imagine that the daily duties of the priestly office in the Church of Rome – such as saying the offices at canonical hours, the hearing of confessions and giving absolutions, without the least dram of labouring in the Word and doctrine – are the means which God has given us in his Word to keep up the power and beauty of Christianity? What these Romish practices do is to effectively keep mankind in sin and security, and men love to have it so.

Many ministers are openly ambitious, insatiably covetous, proud, sensual, haters of those that are good, companions of the worst of men, showing depraved habits of mind.

How dreadfully do such men compare with the apostles and first preachers of the gospel!

May God once again send 'pastors after his own heart to feed the people with knowledge and understanding' (*Jer. 3:15*).

Only the revival of a powerful evangelical ministry will draw the church back from its present apostasy into that glorious state which will truly bring glory to God in the world.

In Jeremiah's day, when the Israelites were rebuked for their sins and warned of God's approaching judgments, they cried, 'The temple of the Lord, the temple of the Lord, the temple of the Lord are these' (*Jer. 7:4*). As if to say, 'You can say what you like, Jeremiah, but we are the only posterity of Abraham, the only church of God in the world. God will never allow his temple and its worship to be destroyed and his people cast out of the land.'

Jeremiah's response was, 'Thus says the Lord of hosts, the God of Israel: "Amend your ways and your doings, and I will cause you to dwell in this place. Do not trust in these lying words, saying, 'The temple of the Lord, the temple of the Lord, the temple of the Lord are these' . . . Behold you trust in lying words that cannot profit. Will you steal, murder, commit adultery, swear falsely, burn incense to Baal, and walk after other gods whom you do not know, and then come and stand before me in this house which is called by my name and say, 'We are delivered to do all these abominations?' . . . But go now to my place which was in Shiloh, where I set my name at the first and see what I did to it because of the wickedness of my people Israel"' (*Jer. 7:3, 4, 8, 9, 10, 12*).

The Israelites were deceived into thinking that it did not matter how they behaved. So long as they were God's people and had the temple and its worship, no judgment could come upon them. The flood of God's judgments could fall on the rest of the world, but they were safe in the ark of the only true church in the world.

John the Baptist also had to deal with this problem. The Pharisees and Sadducees said, 'We have Abraham as our

Father' (*Matt. 3:9*). They thought that because they were the descendants of Abraham, they had an automatic right to all the covenant privileges, however sinful they were in themselves.

It is clear from these examples that the nearer churches or individuals are to God's judgments for their sins, the more ready they are to boast about their church connections and their spiritual privileges, simply because they have nothing else to trust in.

If men were able to excuse their sins under the Old Testament because they considered themselves to be God's special favourites – in spite of Jeremiah's extraordinary prophetic ministry, warning them not to trust in such lies, and calling them instead to repent of their sins and to be holy – how much more will people be able to shelter themselves under similar deceits when they are taught so to do!

When wicked, worldly men, ruled by sinful lusts, are received and welcomed as members of the church of Christ and are made partakers of all outward privileges, it cannot but make them feel safe and weaken all efforts to get them to repent. It also encourages others not to be so watchful and zealous in their Christian lives. After all, when the privilege of having all the outward pledges of God's love and favour can be had on such easy terms and without all the effort of truly repenting and the mortifying of sin, why bother to lead holy lives?

When the church of Sardis was really dead, the best way of keeping it dead was to give it the name of being a really 'live' church (*Rev. 3:1*).

If the church is that society in the world which is the sole object of God's special love and grace; if the chief reason for the administration of its ordinances is to assure men that the benefits of Christ's mediation are for them, how can the lusts of men be more encouraged and condoned than to allow them to partake of these outward privileges whilst they remain unrepentant and continue in their wickedness?

The Lord Christ has made evangelical obedience the outward evidence of being a true member of his church. Obedience to the commands of the gospel is the only indispensable condition of being allowed to participate in the privileges of the gospel. All that is required of us in order that we may be eternally saved is to be found in the gospel commands, 'repent and believe'. And men can have no other outward assurance of their soul's welfare than by being accepted as true members of the church with the right to all its outward privileges.

So when men find that they can easily come by this assurance and all the outward privileges of the church simply by submitting to the ordinances without any true repentance or faith and while they are still continuing to live the most sinful lives, what hope is there of bringing them to true repentance and faith, resulting in holy obedience?

This was how Satan so successfully brought about the general apostasy from evangelical obedience which culminated in the great apostasy of the Church of Rome. Innumerable multitudes were brought to a nominal outward profession of Christianity, not through conviction and personal experience of its truth, power and holiness, leading to present peace and assurance of eternal life, but simply because they wanted to keep in with the rulers of nations and because they were concerned for their own welfare, which was threatened if they did not join the church. In this way, ignorant multitudes were quickly made to feel that they were eternally safe, even though their lives did not come up to the standard of holiness required by the gospel. They were deceitfully assured that although their lives were worse than the lives of the heathen, no matter how lewd, filthy and wicked they were, nevertheless, so long as they were in the Church of

Rome, which alone was the true church of Christ, they were eternally safe and would not perish. Believing this lie, they saw no need why they should trouble themselves with the mortifying of sin, self-denial, purity of heart and hands, and all other gospel duties. So what hope is there of ever expecting holy obedience from such people, who have been given all the privileges of Christianity on such easy terms?

The false assurance into which these ignorant multitudes were led was confirmed when they saw others condemned to eternal hell and consumed by fire and sword in this world simply because they were not, as they were, safe in the ark of the Romish Church. How happy they were and to be congratulated. They were freed from present as well as from eternal flames on such easy terms! And when, to satisfy and pacify guilt, they found relief in confessions, penances, absolutions and redemption of sins by outward works of great piety and charity – which benefited the clergy – as well as the great reserve of purgatory should one die not having sufficiently atoned for any sin, is it any wonder that the majority of men bade farewell to gospel holiness?

By these things, the 'mystery of iniquity' worked until it found its height in the papacy.

The doctrine of the gospel was generally lost through ignorance and errors and it was soon seen how impossible it is to maintain the life and power of obedience when the root of holiness, the doctrines of the gospel are dried up and corrupted. Ignorance of truth and hatred of holiness worked hand in hand to promote the great apostasy.

The ground won by the loss of truth was secured by giving the name, title, privileges and promises of the church to all sorts of men who had never repented of their sins. Assurance was given to the unconverted that they were indeed in that state and condition which the Lord Christ required, even though they continued to lead sinful lives. They were true

Christians, members of Christ's true church even though they gave no evidence of regeneration. When told these things, why bother to seek regeneration and holiness of life? Those who are greatly in love with their sins, lusts and pleasures are not likely to part with them when they are assured of eternal salvation simply by being members of the Church of Rome. And to lead them further into a false sense of security, they are told that the sacraments, solely by virtue of their being administered by a priest, automatically give them all the grace needed for their eternal salvation. In particular, they were taught to believe that everyone who had a mouth, whatever evils may be lodged in the heart and life, might eat the flesh and drink the blood of Jesus Christ and so have eternal life according to Christ's words (*John 6:53, 54*). In these and other ways, the most evil sinners were assured of immortality and glory. Such was the great apostasy of the Church of Rome.

But the Church of Rome went further. To increase the feeling of assurance and comfort, the people were taught that hell and destruction were only for those who were outside the church. 'Outside the Church of Rome there was no salvation.' So, as they were in the church, it did not matter how wicked they were, eternal salvation was theirs. The church was like Noah's ark. All were saved who were in this ark, and all drowned who were outside it. Therefore, they must always keep in the church which alone could preserve them.

Never was there a more wicked scheme invented against the glory of the gospel and evangelical obedience. Professed Christians persecuted, hurt and destroyed others who also professed to be Christians and who were more holy and righteous, but only disagreed with some points of the Christian faith. What can make men feel more secure in their sins than to assure them that they are justified and are more excellent in the eyes of the gospel than those who greatly excel them in morality and holiness? For swearers and drunkards, profane and unclean persons, to cruelly persecute those who are truly holy and seen by men to be sober, self-controlled, prayerful and given to good works, does not put Christianity in a good light!

But if any felt the arrows of conviction and guilt piercing their minds and consciences and troubling them, then confessions, penances and good works would pacify those feelings. And if these were not enough to relieve them of guilt, then purgatory would assuredly do so. So by these wicked doctrines, the majority of Christian mankind were led to despise the gospel and held true gospel holiness in contempt. They did not understand it and nor did they desire it. Instead, a blind devotion, deformed by multiple superstitions, was substituted for gospel holiness. So, under the name of the church and its privileges, the gospel of Christ was utterly lost among men.

The commands of the gospel are most holy, its promises are most glorious and its threatenings most severe. Yet, under a profession of submission to this gospel, men lead lives worse than any heathen who has never known the gospel. To suppose that the gospel encourages evil living is to treat the gospel with the highest and most contemptuous defiance possible.

All this apostasy arises from the belief that so long as I am a member of the Church of Rome and remain so, it does not matter how wickedly I live, I am in the ark and so will never be swept away by the flood of eternal judgment.

The only way back from such apostasy is to so order things in the church that none may flatter themselves that they are true Christians, justified and assured of eternal life, who do not live in subjection to, and in full agreement with, all its commands. But if no more is required to make a Christian than for him to be born in a certain place or nation and to be in the Church of Rome, we must be content to bear the evils of that apostasy under which the world groans.

APOSTASY CAUSED BY PERSONS IN HIGH POSITIONS IN THE CHURCH LEADING EVIL LIVES (*Jer. 23:15*)

The scandalous lives of many popes and prelates in the Church of Rome have driven many to atheism. If religious leaders are not examples of holiness but lead irreligious, immoral, wicked lives, neglect their duties, refuse to rebuke flagrant sins, and yet praise those who do such sins, then a whole generation of professed Christians will soon be influenced, corrupted and depraved. What will the household be like when the stewards are evil? (*Matt. 24:48–51*).

As the people in the Church of Rome are warned not to be wiser than their teachers, but faithfully to obey their priests and to follow their examples, so they either cannot or will not, for the most part, see any reason why they should be better than their priests or walk in any other paths than those their leaders tread before them.

Under the Old Testament the sons of Eli, the high priest, lived profane and immoral lives, and as a result the majority of the nation was soon corrupted and the judgments of God soon followed (*1 Sam. 2:12–17*).

So the great apostasy of the Church of Rome was promoted by the open pride, ambition, strife, contentions and conformity to the world of its prelates and popes after it came under the protection of the Roman empire.

Men bought the privileges of the church for themselves by giving wealth and honour to persons in no way better than themselves, but who held the name and title of 'clergy' or 'guides of the church'. And when things grew worse and worse in the Church of Rome, the lewd, wicked lives of popes, prelates and others, made worse by their high positions of power and dignity, led the people into every form of corruption and degradation.

The world judges the church by its leaders and guides. So they must be examples of eminent holiness. They must show forth in their lives the grace of the gospel in all humility and meekness. They must show contempt for the world, its sensual pleasures and the pride of life. They must preach the Word with all zeal and diligence. Otherwise, apostasy from the power and holiness of the gospel will continue to go from bad to worse.

APOSTASY PROMOTED BY PERSECUTIONS

I do not mean that persecution which Christians are warned to expect from the world and which has never been the cause of apostasy but rather has redounded to the glory of the church, but those horribly cruel persecutions of humble, godly Christians by the Church of Rome. This was foretold in the Book of Revelation. In that book is prophesied a cruel, apostate church which would persecute, destroy and kill all who did not submit to her in her apostasy. Because of its idolatry as well as its cruelty, this apostate church is called Babylon. And we are told that, when Babylon is destroyed, 'in her was found the blood of the prophets and of saints, and of all that were slain on the earth', slain because they were faithful to the gospel of Christ (*Rev. 18:24*). So anyone who persecutes a person because of his faith in the gospel of Christ, whatever excuses he might make, joins himself to that apostate church which one day is destined to be utterly destroyed.

Our Lord Jesus Christ came to restore that love of God which had departed from our human nature. He came to save the lives of men, not to destroy them. He came to deliver them from a state of enmity and mutual hatred into a state of peace and love. Can any sane man, then, imagine that

hurting, imprisoning, fining, banishing, killing and destroying men for no other reason than their faith in Christ and their
worshipping of Christ in the way they are convinced they
ought to worship Christ, truly shows the glory of Christ, the
Prince of peace and love? Does it not rather teach that
Christianity is fierce, cruel, oppressive, vindictive and
bloody?

So when mankind, by what they saw and heard, were
persuaded that this was the true religion and that it taught men
to persecute and destroy those who did not agree with it, then
they had truly lost the gospel and all its benefits. But this
persecuting religion, rather than showing itself to be Christ's
true religion, shows itself to be the religion of antichrist. And
when at any time this kind of persecution prevails amongst
Christians, then there is left no form, face or appearance of
Christianity among men. All that love, charity, peace, meekness, quietness, mercy, compassion and kindness towards all
mankind, which are the true credentials of gospel believers,
give way to wrath, strife, revenge, evil surmises, false accusa-
tions, tumults, disorders, force and everything that is evil.

Whatever advantages any shall pretend have been brought
to the church by these persecutions, certainly they have been a
thousand times more advantageous to the forces of error by the
corruption of Christian morality.

APOSTASY SUPPORTED AND PROMOTED BY NATIONAL SINS
'Everybody does it!' The best evidence that the preaching of
the gospel has been widely accepted in the nation may be seen
by the success it has in subduing national sins. If national sins
are not to some extent subdued; if the minds of men are not
turned from them and made watchful against them; if the guilt
of these sins is not accepted, and if excuses are made for them,
such as 'everybody does it', whatever profession the nation
makes of being Christian is vain and useless.

Paul declared that the national sin of the Cretans was that of telling lies (*Titus 1:12, 13*). So whatever profession the Cretans might make of being a Christian nation, if they continued to be liars, their profession would be false and the gospel would not have been received in life-giving power. Whatever their profession of Christianity, if people are not delivered from national sins, they will not long remain sound in the faith, nor will they be fruitful in obedience.

The national sin of the Jews was stubbornness and obstinacy, of which God continually complained. So good King Josiah was commended 'because his heart was tender' (*2 Chron. 34:27*). Josiah was not held under the power of the common sin of the people. The commendation was all the greater because it was rare to find one with a tender heart.

And what shall we say is the common sin of our nation? Is it not the gratification of our sensual appetites, 'eating, drinking and being merry'? And like that foolish farmer in Christ's parable, all our labour is to satisfy our sensual lusts and pleasures (*Luke 12:13–21*).

Has the gospel delivered us from this sin? Only by putting on 'the whole armour of God' can we defend ourselves against this national sin.

In Isaiah's day it was difficult for individuals to stand alone against the tide of opinion. People were afraid of standing alone for that which they knew to be right. But the few who did, such as Isaiah and his family, were treated as objects of contempt and ridicule, as 'signs and wonders in Israel' (*Isa. 8:11–18*). Only by making God their 'fear and dread' were they able to overcome the fear of being mocked and jeered at by the crowd.

Some are led into national sins by a corrupt education; others by laziness, negligence and a false sense of security. Some indulge in national sins because 'everybody does them'.

National sins turn people away from gospel obedience. And if these national sins are excused and indulged in by those who profess to be Christians, then is Christianity, as far as customs, manners, vanities, vices and living are concerned, dragged down to the level of heathenism. National sins eat out the heart and power of Christianity, leaving only the outward show of a form of godliness.

The Christian gospel was designed to turn men from 'all ungodliness and worldly lusts, to live soberly, righteously and godly in this present world'. And where this is not done, then either the gospel has not been generally received or else men have fallen away from it.

The gospel comes on a nation like a farmer working on a wilderness or forest that is full of thorns and briers because of the poverty of the soil. There it uproots and burns the thorns and briers, replanting with good and noble plants instead. Soon the barren wilderness becomes a fruitful field. But in time, if there is no continual care and culture, the earth of its own accord begins to grow the weeds, thorns and briers natural to it. These, springing up abundantly, choke the good plants and so in time the fruitful field returns to being a barren wilderness.

So, no more is needed to promote apostasy than to allow national vices, for a time suppressed by the power of the gospel, to once again take fast hold of the hearts of the people and so stifle and choke the graces of the gospel.

APOSTASY CAUSED BY MISTAKES ABOUT THE BEAUTY AND GLORY OF THE CHRISTIAN RELIGION

Under the Old Testament, the glory of true religion was in its temple, its sacrifices and the garments of the high priest. All these things were visible to the eye.

Under the New Testament, the glory of true religion lay in the internal work of the Holy Spirit, renewing our natures, transforming us into the image and likeness of God, producing the fruits of his grace in a righteous and holy life. Meekness, humility and graciousness were the marks of true Christian behaviour. But few are able to discern the beauty, glory or honour in these things. And where the spiritual glory of the gospel is not seen, then, of necessity, it is despised and abandoned, and something else put in its place. And what is put in its place is something invented by man and so apostasy from gospel holiness is promoted.

Men naturally can see no more beauty in the spiritual power of Christianity than the Jews could see in the person of Christ when they rejected him (*Isa. 53:2*). So leaving the wisdom of God declared in Scripture, they substituted their own inventions.

Instead of the ministry of the church being humble, holy, hardworking, filled with the graces and gifts of the Spirit, looking for no honour or respect from the world, but only that honour which comes from God, it became pompous, ambitious and dressed in gorgeous worldly vestments nowhere prescribed by the Word of God. And instead of a worship, simple, unadorned and spiritual – whose life and excellence lay in the invisible, effectual work of the Holy Spirit, showing itself in meekness, self-denial, mortification of sin and the fruits of righteousness, all arising from the gracious work of the Holy Spirit – they substituted forms of outward, visible worship which was more acceptable in the world, but nowhere prescribed by Christ.

So the glory of Christianity was now corrupted by the pompous grandeur of the priests of the church, along with a pompous, ceremonious worship awash with superstitions and idolatry. The people continued to live sinful lives and quietened their consciences by enriching the church, so benefiting the clergy with magnificent, generous buildings and gifts.

Once the world was persuaded that these things were the true glory of the Christian religion, and that they allowed a person to continue to indulge his lusts and sins, then real holiness and obedience was more and more neglected and despised. But there was still worse to come. Amongst the clergy arose jealousies and ambitious quarrels about who should hold what positions of importance in the church, which led the heathen to despise Christianity as a depraved and corrupt religion.

APOSTASY BROUGHT ABOUT BY THE GREAT APOSTATE HIMSELF

The devil, that greatest of all apostates, has it as his chief desire to destroy Christ's church on earth, and failing that, to utterly corrupt it and so make it his church.

As a lion, the devil raged against the church with bloody and violent persecutions. But failing to destroy it, he crept into the church as a poisonous serpent. Once in, he secretly and gradually poisoned the minds of many by vain thoughts of power and ambition, with love for the praise and honours of the world, and with superstitions. Thus, he turned them from the spiritual power and simplicity of the gospel, deceiving them as he deceived Eve in the beginning (*2 Cor. 11:3*). Sometimes he 'transformed himself into an angel of light' (*2 Cor. 11:14, 15*). The devil not only poisoned and inflamed the lusts of men, but drew them away from the gospel by suggestions and pretence of more piety and devotion. In this way, the 'mystery of iniquity' worked and was successful (*2 Thess. 2:7*).

So successful was the devil's work that, on the one hand, Christians were given up to the power of sensual lusts, or brought up under the power of superstitions. But when men gave themselves up to his delusions, rejecting the truth and holiness of the gospel, God gave them up to the devil's power, to be deceived and hardened to their eternal ruin

(*2 Thess. 2:11, 12*). So the apostasy came to its final fulfilment under the papacy. And by the same deceits, Satan still works in churches today, leading them back into that great apostasy from which they had been delivered at the Reformation.

APOSTASY CAUSED BY DIVISIONS IN THE CHURCH AND BY THE USELESSNESS OF CHRISTIANS

The Lord Jesus Christ told his disciples that all would know that they were his disciples if they loved one another (*John 13:35*). This was to be the great testimony to the reality of their faith in him, his doctrine and the sincerity of their obedience. It was for this genuine unity and love amongst his disciples that Christ prayed (*John 17:20, 21*).

The happy effects and fruits of these commands were great for a while among those who professed the gospel, and their mutual love was a convincing argument for the truth, power and holiness of the doctrine they professed. Where there is unity and love, there is peace, order, usefulness and every good work. But where these are lacking, there is strife, envy, confusion, disorder and every evil work.

Some early Christians fell out with each other, but these quarrels were quickly healed by the spirit of apostolic authority and that love which prevailed among them (*Acts 11:1–18; 15:1–29*).

But later, things grew worse and the first visible signs of degeneracy in Christianity were seen in the strifes, divisions and quarrels between Christians, especially between their leaders. These divisions and strifes were carried on with such an evil spirit of pride, ambition, envy and malice that even the heathen joked about them and declared that there were no other men in the world so ready as Christians to argue and refuse to listen to the other person's point of view.

But when one party got into power, they snatched the sword of violence out of the hands of paganism, which had already been stained with the blood of the holy martyrs, and began to persecute with great cruelty Christians who did not agree with them. And it was only by the unspeakable care and mercy of God that the gospel was not hated by all men as the cause of all this malice and hatred.

But is it not the same today amongst those who claim the strictest adherence to the truth of the gospel? Do not some seem to have nothing else to do but to create divisions? Some seem to delight in nothing more than to live and dispute in the flames of these divisions. Divisions arise at the least theological difference between Christians. Because of this, Christianity has lost much of that awesome authority in the world by which it has often been the means of great restraint on the minds and consciences of men who have never tasted the real power of the gospel.

Great offence is given to the world also by the uselessness of Christians. Christians ought to be a blessing to everybody. But they are not.

There is a selfish spirit in many Christians. Contenting themselves with abstaining from sins and with divine worship, they are of little or no use to others. Some will be kind, helpful and good to a limited extent. They are concerned only for their own household or their own church. But as for love, concern, generosity, kindness, readiness to help all, even the worst of men, as they are able, it is scarcely to be found among Christians. Every excuse is made to justify this lack of Christian love. But if we are Christians, we are 'to abound in love to all' (*1 Thess. 3:12*).

Our doing good to all, being useful to all, exercising lovingkindness to all is the chief way by which we may show our sincere obedience to the gospel. One such Christian is worth more to the gospel than thousands who live only to themselves.

If the world cannot see any good coming from Christians, but sees only hatred and strife, then it is no wonder that it has no desire for fellowship with us. If men saw that when any are converted to Christ, they immediately become kind, merciful, charitable and good to all men, it could not but leave a favourable impression.

TO SUM UP

All who profess to be Christians but are not living holy lives are really renouncing obedience to Christ's commands and despising his promises, preferring instead the pleasures of sin. Such people declare that they have found nothing lovely in Christ's commands, nor any happiness in keeping them, nor any assurance in Christ's promises, nor any value in the things promised compared with the world and the pleasures of sin.

So some commands of the gospel, such as an active, mutual love, are rejected and replaced with a passive harmlessness. 'I try not to do anybody any harm.' But that watchfulness over one another with love, care and tenderness, along with mutual warnings, exhortations and comforts which the gospel so frequently and diligently puts to us, are not only neglected, but so greatly despised that the very mention of these duties is treated with contempt and scorned as mere hypocrisy. How can greater dishonour and contempt be cast upon Christ?

By continuing in the outward profession of Christianity, hypocrites falsely represent Christ and the gospel to the world and so 'put him to an open shame'. By continuing in sin and pretending obedience to Christ, and that in Christ they have placed their hope for life and eternal blessedness, they declare that he approves of their sin and that his gospel allows and excuses such evil living.

Our Lord Jesus Christ instituted a solemn worship of God to be continued without alteration to the end of the world. The chief reason why he created and preserves his church is so that this worship is celebrated. This is that public glory which God requires from believers in this world. All other duties could be carried out by men on their own, even if there were no such thing as a church. That church, therefore, which does not take care that the worship which Christ appointed is duly celebrated has not understood the chief reason for its existence.

Apostasy from evangelical worship happens in two ways. It happens either by neglecting and refusing to observe what Christ has appointed, or by adding ways of worshipping which we have invented.

Some have fallen away from the worship of the gospel by only doing some things which have an appearance of that which Christ has commanded. They are led by what they consider convenient and by their inner light. But the sacraments of baptism and the Lord's supper, which are so great a part of the mystical worship of the church, they reject.

The chief reason why some have forsaken the sacraments is because they do not represent that false faith and obedience which they have substituted for the true faith and gospel obedience.

The sacraments of the gospel represent to us, by outward, visible signs, the gospel doctrines which we believe. Baptism represents regeneration. But if we do not believe there is such a spiritual work as regeneration and do not see any need for such a work, then baptism becomes meaningless and will be forsaken.

The sacrament of the Lord's supper represents to us, by outward, visible signs, the death of Christ. It calls us to remember his suffering in our place for our sins; the sacrifice he made of himself; the atonement or reconciliation with God that he wrought and the sealing of the new covenant with his blood. But if we reject these doctrines, then this sacrament becomes meaningless and is rejected also.

Only when the doctrines of the gospel are truly believed will these sacraments be a delight and a joy and become the means by which Christ has fellowship with his people, bringing comfort, peace and assurance to their hearts.

Another reason why the sacraments of the gospel are forsaken is the lack of spiritual illumination to see through the veils of the outward, visible signs to the spiritual realities which they signify, and the lack of the wisdom of faith to have communion with God in Christ by them.

Gospel worship is purely spiritual. But in the sacraments there are elements which are outward and visible, and it is to be feared that many go no further than sight and taste, and do not enter into the spiritual worship of God by them. But they are appointed by Christ to lead the soul into intimate communion with God.

If we are, therefore, to profit spiritually by the use of these sacraments, we must submit our souls and consciences to the authority of Christ in them. We must trust in the faithfulness of Christ, that he will bring to our souls the grace and mercy represented by the signs and sacramentally exhibited by them. The sacraments will not profit those who do not by faith receive the promises which Christ has joined to them, and we cannot believe the promise, unless we submit to the authority of Christ in the sacrament.

We must understand to some extent the mystical union

that is between the outward, visible signs and the Lord Christ himself if we are to benefit from the use of the sacraments and conscientiously continue to use them.

But where there is no understanding, and no faith in the doctrines they represent, then it is no wonder that they are forsaken and people fall away from the true, spiritual worship of the gospel, bringing great dishonour to the Son of God, the author and Lord of all evangelical worship.

There is another way by which men fall away from evangelical worship, and that is by rejecting its simplicity and its pure institutions, for a superstitious, idolatrous worship (*2 Cor. 11:3*). There are degrees of apostasy from true and pure gospel worship. But in the Church of Rome, true evangelical worship has been totally perverted and corrupted. There is not one single ordinance or institution of Christ which they have not corrupted, and most of them are so far corrupted as to utterly destroy their nature and their original intention.

In giving the church such ordinances, the Lord Jesus Christ shows that it is his religion and that he alone has authority over it. So, to remove Christ's ordinances and to introduce them in another form and for an entirely different purpose is to declare oneself to be antichrist, and so put Christ to an open shame. This the Roman Catholic Church has done, and so has declared itself to be antichrist.

As men grew carnal, having lost the spirit, life and power of the gospel, they found it necessary to introduce a carnal, visible, pompous, outward worship, as did the Israelites in the wilderness when they made the golden calf, saying to Aaron, 'Make us gods who will go before us – gods we can see.'

So in the great Christian apostasy, finding all the outward, visible signs of Old Testament worship taken away, and being now left with no visible images of God's presence, superstitious and idolatrous calves were set up, suited to carnal, unspiritual worship. Such is the worship instituted and invented by the Church of Rome.

But because many in those days were truly spiritual and holy, who worshipped God in Spirit and in truth, this idolatrous worship could only be introduced slowly and over a long period of time. Thus the 'mystery of iniquity' worked to destroy true and pure evangelical worship.

12: *The Dangers of Widespread Apostasy*

'Let him that thinks he stands take heed lest he fall' (*1 Cor. 10:12*).

Paul reminds the Roman Christians of the Jewish apostasy, which was why God had cut them off. The Gentiles were now grafted in in place of the Jews, and because of that, they were beginning to boast against the Jews because they were now given pride of place over them.

Paul says, 'Do not boast against the branches. But if you boast, remember that you do not support the root, but the root supports you. You will say then, "Branches were broken off that I might be grafted in." Well said. Because of unbelief they were broken off, and you stand by faith. Do not be haughty, but fear. For if God did not spare the natural branches, he may not spare you either' (*Rom. 11:18–21*).

Some think that the preservation of true religion is the work of the appointed ministry. So they are not worried. It is not their concern.

But every Christian is responsible to see that the power and truth of holiness is kept up in his own heart and life. Only then will apostasy be restrained. For if the people are not holy, then churches will not be holy and nor will nations.

Others do not deny the present widespread apostasy, but they are certain that they will not fall away from the gospel. Others need to be warned, but not they.

These forget the example of Peter. He did not think that he would ever deny Christ. But how wrong he was! Later, in writing his first letter, he warns Christians not to live presumptuously, as if they could never fall away. They must not only live their lives in fear but also sanctify the Lord God in their hearts, and always be ready to give a reason for the hope that is in them with meekness and fear (*1 Pet. 1:17; 3:14, 15*).

WARNING ONE

Consider how widespread this apostasy is. Ignorance, profaneness and worldly-mindedness show how people have forsaken the Lord; how sinful the nation is; how its people are laden with iniquity; how they have provoked the Lord to anger (*Isa. 1:4–6*).

If we are warned that there is an epidemic in the land and that one or two people have died of it, we are rightly concerned and take precautions so that we are not infected with it. But if the epidemic is widespread throughout the land and thousands are dying because of it, we would indeed be foolish if we lived presumptuously, believing that we alone would be spared even if we took no precautions.

Many are being hardened through 'the deceitfulness of sin'. Are we not in danger of being hardened also? Our souls have in them the same principles – sin and love of the world – as well as those who have fallen away from Christ. Are we better and stronger than they to resist the temptations to apostatize? We are fools if we do not stir ourselves up to greater watchfulness in this time of great spiritual danger.

WARNING TWO

The present widespread apostasy has a great danger attached to it.

When an epidemic is on the wane, the danger of contracting the infection is not considered to be so great. But when the epidemic is spreading rapidly, then the danger is great.

Today, all are agreed that the state of the world is getting worse and worse. What evidences have we of great revivals which are turning nations to the gospel and its peoples to holy living?

The majority in our nation rejects true religion. Rome's influence is greatly increasing. Biblical truth loses ground every day whilst heretical cults grow and increase.

Is this a time to be secure and careless? Can we find no incipient apostasy in ourselves? Is there no decay in zeal and love in our hearts? Have we never neglected Christian duties? Is there no lukewarmness in us and in our churches? (*Rev. 3:15–17*). Have we a name to live, but in reality are spiritually dead or near to death? (*Rev. 3:1*).

The great danger of this apostasy is that it comes in such a way as to make Christians and churches feel that it is not spreading and increasing, but that it is on the way out.

WARNING THREE

We do not know how far this apostasy will spread and to what heights it will reach. God can put a stop to it at any moment. But, provoked by the ingratitude of a wicked world, not one of us knows how long God will withhold the powerful influences of his Spirit. The whole world, as far as we know, may become papal, aided and abetted by those who claim to adhere to biblical truth, or else become so corrupt that it does not make much difference what their religion is.

But there are two truths that can bring us comfort in this time of widespread apostasy:

The first truth is, 'The Lord knows those who are his' (*2 Tim. 2:19*). His elect will be preserved and will never be allowed to fall away into irrecoverable apostasy.

The second truth is that God has appointed a time when he will put a stop to all apostasy and 'the earth will be filled with the knowledge of the glory of the Lord as the waters cover the sea' (*Hab. 2:14*).

He will one day pour out his judgment plagues on Babylon, and the kingdoms of the world will become the kingdoms of our Lord and of his Christ, and he shall reign for ever and ever (*Rev. 11:15*). But when these things will be, and what will happen until they are fulfilled, we do not know. Therefore, we are to watch lest we too be overtaken by this great apostasy.

WARNING FOUR

Consider how insidiously and deceitfully this apostasy intrudes into the lives of the people, leading them away from the gospel.

Apostasy has many subtle, insidious ways of deceiving unstable souls. It may get at us in our work, at home through the family, in our pleasures or by means of our possessions.

Unbelief, the deceitfulness of sin, corrupt lusts and desires, spiritual laziness, the love of money and its attendant worries, all lie ready to entice us away from the gospel into apostasy. Therefore we must 'lay aside every weight and the sin which so easily ensnares us' (*Heb. 12:1*). We are to 'beware lest there be in any of us an evil heart of unbelief in departing from the living God'. We are to 'exhort one another daily, lest any of us be hardened through the deceitfulness of sin' (*Heb. 3:12, 13*). We must 'pursue peace with all men, and holiness, without which no one will see the Lord: looking diligently lest anyone should fall short of the grace of God; lest any root of bitterness springing up should cause trouble, and by this many become defiled; lest there be any fornicator or profane person like Esau, who for one morsel of food sold his birthright. For you know that afterwards, when he wanted to inherit the blessing, he was rejected, for he found no place for repentance, though he sought it diligently with tears' (*Heb. 12:14–17*).

Satan waits to corrupt our minds and poison our lusts. He is like a roaring lion, seeking whom he may devour (*2 Cor. 11:3; 1 Pet. 5:8*).

Some fall into apostasy by 'damnable heresies, denying the Lord that bought them' (*2 Pet. 2:1*). Some are led into apostasy by superstition and idolatry and some by contempt of gospel mysteries. Ambition, pride, love of the world, neglect of spiritual and moral duties, carnal wisdom, sensual lusts, doubt and indifference to supernatural and divine things, the praise and popularity of the world with its vain pomp and spectacles, leading people to love pleasure more than God, are all ways by which apostasy dangerously infects and deceives people.

So we are not to be deceived. 'Evil company corrupts good habits' (*1 Cor. 15:33*).

Snakes and scorpions lie everywhere at our feet. Snares and traps are laid for us. Those who escape one evil are in danger of falling into others. How shall we escape falling into apostasy if we neglect even one duty?

WARNING FIVE

There is an apostasy which is irrecoverable and which ends in eternal ruin for souls.

No-one, according to the rule of the gospel, can be in a state where he cannot be saved. God does not allow any man to be the absolute sovereign judge of himself, which would usurp his divine prerogative and put the sinner in the place of God himself. He that despairs says, 'I am my own God in this matter. I have greatly sinned and have judged myself to have eternally forfeited salvation. I cannot see how the goodness of God can possibly show any grace or mercy to me.' This evil attitude God has rebuked by wonderfully saving great apostates. We think especially of King Manasseh (*2 Chron. 33:10–13*).

Nevertheless, there is an apostasy from which it is impossible for a person to be restored and recovered.

There is that apostasy where the means of grace can only

produce the weeds and thorns of unbelief and rejection of the gospel (*Heb. 6:4–8*). And there is that apostasy where the great salvation is wilfully neglected and despised in its ordinances (*Heb. 10:26–29*).

All backslidings, if we are not careful, can lead to this state of irrecoverable apostasy. Therefore, we must take heed that we do not ride with the hounds of any one sin, nor embrace one sinful lust.

WARNING SIX

Consider the nature and guilt of total apostasy and the severity of God against such apostates.

Total apostasy from Christ and the gospel is a greater sin than that of the Jews in crucifying Christ. The Jews who crucified Christ had the gospel preached to them and many repented and received the gospel and so were eternally saved. But God has no further gospel to preach to those who totally reject it, and he has no other Christ to atone for their apostasy. Therefore, there is no possibility of salvation for such apostates.

DANGER SIGNS OF ENCROACHING TOTAL APOSTASY

Sign one. The loss of all appreciation of the goodness, excellence and glories of the truth of the gospel is the first warning sign. As the Jews saw nothing in Christ which could make them desire him, so the person heading for total apostasy begins to see nothing in the gospel that he should desire it. Along with this sign there is a love of sin and of the pleasures of this world. Delight in Christ and his gospel is dulled, if not totally lost.

Sign two. The first sign is quickly followed by the loss of conviction that the gospel is true and comes from God. The evidences which God has put into the gospel to prove the truth of its divine origin and all arguments for its truth no longer make any impression or have any authority. The gospel is now looked on as a 'cunningly devised fable'. No longer is assent given to its truth and the person becomes an unbeliever. He has no more respect for Scripture.

Sign three. Contempt for the things promised in the gospel follows. Out of hatred for Jesus Christ, the apostate rejects and despises the promises and eternally deprives his soul of them. He would rather not have God than have him by Christ. This is the most provoking of sins. No greater reproach can possibly rest on Christ than that which leaves him neither the honour of his truth nor the honour of his power. Of neither of these sins could the Jews who crucified Christ be accused.

Sign four. The apostate may totally reject the Christian religion for another religion, or partially reject the gospel and the purity of gospel worship for the superstitious doctrines and the idolatrous worship of Rome. This brings great dishonour to Christ, who so graciously delivered us from these evils at the Reformation. Or else the apostate rejects God totally, no longer seeking in any way at all to please him or live to him. His god now is his own lusts and desires. He lives solely for the pleasures of the world, preferring them to Christ and his promises and contemptuously despises all his threatenings (*Phil. 3:18, 19*).

Sign five. Rejecting Christ and his pure religion, the apostate also despises and rejects Christ's faithful people. Great apostates have always been great persecutors, both in word and deed, according to their power and ability.

All who love Christ love his people also. Those who hate Christ also hate all who are his. They are despised as weak and foolish to continue to believe the gospel. So the apostate leaves the fellowship of Christians (*1 John 2:19*).

Sign six. Finally, they despise the Spirit of God and his whole work in the gospel dispensation (*Heb. 10:29*).

The Holy Spirit is the One specially promised for the gospel era. This promise of the Holy Spirit is the special privilege and glory of the gospel. He was sent by the risen and exalted Christ (*Acts 2:33*). His whole work is to glorify and exalt Christ and to make his mediatorial work effective in the souls of men. The Holy Spirit is the life and soul of the gospel.

Therefore, apostasy from the gospel shows special enmity against him and his work.

When apostates have 'trampled the Son of God underfoot' and 'counted the blood of the covenant by which he was sanctified a common thing', then they will and do 'insult the Spirit of grace' (*Heb. 10:29*).

Sign seven. Total apostasy shows itself in the open profession and declaration of hatred against the gospel so far as is consistent with worldly interests. Secular interests may not make it wise or feasible to openly reveal that one has totally renounced Christ and his gospel. But when apostasy is widespread and the popular thing to do, then the apostate will unashamedly reveal his true, traitorous colours.

These, then, are the seven signs of total apostasy to which we would do well to take heed.

Total apostasy makes it inconsistent with the holiness, righteousness and faithfulness of God to renew to repentance such persons who are fully and openly guilty of such a sin. Some men who have tried the truths of the gospel and had some convictions of its truth and excellence obstinately reject the only way of salvation that God has provided for sinners – and so have despised the whole blessed Trinity, each divine person in his part of the work of salvation. God in his faithfulness neither will, nor in his holiness can, have any mercy on such presumptuous sinners. God may and does put up with wicked apostates for a while in this world, and that without any visible signs of his displeasure, satisfying his justice in the spiritual judgments that lie upon them. But God only tolerates them 'as vessels of wrath prepared for destruction' and whose 'destruction does not slumber' (*Rom. 9:22; 2 Pet. 2:3*). And these things may be sufficient to warn men of the danger of apostasy. They will be warnings to all who consider them, who are not yet hardened 'through the deceitfulness of sin'.

To those who fear that they might have sunk into the state of irrecoverable apostasy because they feel spiritually dead and barren and have neglected spiritual duties because of sinful pleasures and are in a state of despair, I offer the following.

All backslidings are perilous. Whilst in such a state, none can have an assurance of peace and comfort from God and his promises. Therefore, repent and 'seek the Lord while he may be found, call upon him while he is near. Let the wicked forsake his way, and the unrighteous man his thoughts; let him return to the Lord, and he will have mercy upon him; and to our God, for he will abundantly pardon' (*Isa. 55:6, 7*).

If you are spiritually aware of the evil of your backsliding, then you are still in a recoverable condition. No-one is past hope of salvation until he is past all possibility of repentance. And no-one is past all possibility of repentance until he is absolutely hardened against all gospel convictions.

Christ calls men back from their backslidings and will help those who wholeheartedly seek him (*Rev. 2:5; 3:1–3*).

God has promised to restore and heal such backslidings in believers (*Hos. 14:4*).

If these are not sufficient to encourage you to repent of your backslidings, then it is to be feared you will become worse and worse through the power of sin until it has full dominion over you. Whatever excuses you make for not repenting, the truth is that you will not repent, either because of unbelief or because you love the pleasures of sin more than you love God.

So, if your backsliding from the ways of holiness and obedience has not arisen from a dislike of Christ and the gospel, and if you have not chosen any other religion or sin in preference to Christ, then you have every encouragement to repent and the use of all gospel means is yours to bring you to a blessed recovery. But the command to repent is urgent, as was the command to Lot to leave Sodom (*Gen. 19:15, 16*). It is not the time to linger and to think about it. There is no time for delay.

'But what about my continued and repeated failures? I have never lived up to the standard of holiness required by the gospel, so my condition is the same as those who have fallen from gospel holiness. Sin has dominion over me. I am continually being overcome by one sin and now it has become a habit.'

There are three things you need to know about the power of sin:

First, there is the captivating power of sin (*Rom. 7:23*). Under sin's captivating power, the will in all its desires and inclinations is dead set against the power of sin, so that in all its struggles it suffers hardship because it is aware of its captivity to sin. This captivity to the law of sin does not mean the person actually commits sin, but refers only to the struggle against sin that goes on in his mind and heart. From this condition, no-one is perfectly freed whilst he is still in this world (*Rom. 7:24*).

Second, there is the 'overcoming power of sin' (*2 Pet. 2:19*). Men are 'servants of corruption' in that they are 'overcome' by sin and 'brought into bondage'. They do not willingly give themselves up to the service of sin but are overcome by its power.

Third, there is a state of sin in which men, being wholly

under its power, willingly give themselves up to its service in spite of pangs of conscience (*Rom. 6:16, 19*).

So those who complain they are under the power of some habit of sin which they cannot overcome seem to be such who, notwithstanding all their light and conviction, with all the efforts they make, are so far under the power of some sin as to be in its service, frequently committing actual sins.

If this is the case, then they are in great danger. If some cure is not found, they will never have any assurance that they are true Christians.

If you are such a person and have tried and failed to break this sinful habit, seek some able, spiritual person who can help you.

'Confess your trespasses to one another' (*James 5:16*). By Satan's craft, this ordinance was abused by turning it into a necessary confession of all sin to a priest supposedly invested with the power of absolution. This brought about innumerable evils and ruined the souls of men by keeping them away from the true purpose of this injunction, which was for Christians to seek help from one another.

'And if your right eye causes you to sin, pluck it out and cast it from you; for it is more profitable for you that one of your members perish, than for your whole body to be cast into hell. And if your right hand causes you to sin, cut it off and cast it from you; for it is more profitable for you that one of your members perish, than for your whole body to be cast into hell' (*Matt. 5:29, 30*).

You must take hold of this sinful habit and pluck it out of your life. You must cut it off and cast it from you. You must reject its first temptations. Treat it as some thief or person bent on evil who wishes you to join with him. Do not give your consent (*Psa. 50:18; Prov. 1:10–19*). Reject it as an alcoholic must reject wine (*Prov. 23:31*). Reject it as a moral man rejects an immoral woman (*Prov. 5*).

All reasons why this habit must be spared must also be rejected. Avoid all places and people where this sin is allowed and where it would be difficult for you to resist it (*Prov. 4:14, 15*).

Finally, pray without ceasing for grace to overcome the power of this habit.

When Moses' hands were down, Amalek prevailed. But when Moses' hands were up, Amalek was defeated (*Exod. 17:11*).

This sinful habit is your Amalek, and may be the means God is using to teach you the power of prayer and to get you into the habit of prayer. It may also be your 'thorn in the flesh' to keep you humble with a sense of your weakness, and so dependent on the grace of Christ (*2 Cor. 12:7–10*).

13: *Defences Against Apostasy*

If we would defend ourselves against all temptations to apostasy, then we must first be concerned for the glory of God

When God threatened to cast off the Israelites in the wilderness because of their unbelief and refusal to enter Canaan, Moses showed how concerned he was for the glory of God's holy name. If God cast off his people, what would the other nations say? They would say that God cast them off because he was not able to keep his promise to bring them into the land of Canaan (*Numb. 14:11–19*).

It was the same with Joshua when, after the miraculous overthrow of Jericho, the Israelite army was defeated at Ai. How concerned he was for the glory of God's name.

'O Lord,' Joshua prayed, 'what shall I say when Israel turns its back before its enemies? For the Canaanites and all the inhabitants of the land will hear of it, and surround us, and cut off our name from the earth. Then what will you do for your great name?' (*Josh. 7:8, 9*).

This widespread apostasy is greatly dishonouring to the glory of God's great name. Who will glorify the great name of God if all his faithful people fall away into apostasy?

How many nations that were once receptive to the gospel are now overrun by Islam, paganism and atheism? How concerned are we for the glory of God's holy name?

Thousands in our own nation who call themselves Christians are so in name only. They have an outward form of godliness but there is no reality in their lives. So they bring the Christian religion into contempt in the eyes of the world. How concerned are we about this? Is not God's glorious name dishonoured by such widespread hypocrisy? Is God's name glorified when so many in our churches have fallen away from the doctrines, the worship and the obedience of the gospel?

Are we not concerned that so many Christians are falling away from the truth of the gospel and returning to the superstitions and idolatries of Rome? Is this glorifying to God's name?

Should we not sigh and cry over all these abominations (*Ezek. 9:4*)? Or have we Gallio's attitude of not caring about these things (*Acts 18:17*)?

God set a mark on all those who cried and sighed over all the abominations which were being committed in Jerusalem and in the temple. These people came under God's special protection and care when his judgments went through the land. So if we are concerned for the glory of God's holy name and mourn in secret over the abominable apostasy which, like a deadly epidemic, is destroying the spiritual lives of thousands and dishonouring God's holy name, then we too shall be under his special care and protection, and he will keep us safe when apostasy seeks to tempt us away from the gospel. His mark will be upon us.

If we would defend ourselves from all temptations to apostasy, then we must pray continually, pleading the promises recorded in God's Word for the restoration of the glory, power and purity of the Christian religion

We must be like watchmen on the walls of Jerusalem who never hold their peace day or night. We who make mention of the Lord must not keep silent, and nor must we give God any rest until he makes the Christian gospel a praise in all the earth (*Isa. 62:6, 7*).

There is nothing too hard for God. He can send peace, truth and righteousness in the world. He can rain down righteousness until the earth opens and brings forth salvation (*Isa. 45:8*). Were this left to the depraved wills of men, there would be no end to this apostasy. Only sovereign, effectual grace can stop this apostasy and bring about a great revival.

If we would defend ourselves from all temptations to apostasy, then we must contend earnestly for the faith which was once for all delivered to the saints (Jude 3)

We must not be put off by the contempt and scorn which the world and apostates pour on evangelical truth. We must give faithful testimony to it, not only by our words, but by our lives also. We must live holy, righteous and fruitful lives, 'having a good conscience, that when they defame us as evil-doers, those who revile our good conduct in Christ may be ashamed' (*1 Pet. 3:16*).

If we would defend ourselves from all temptations to apostasy, we must keep a careful watch over our own hearts

'Keep your heart with all diligence, for out of it spring the issues of life' (*Prov. 4:23*). This was Solomon's advice. And this should be our greatest concern. It is more important to keep our hearts safe in the truths of the gospel than to keep our possessions safe in a secure house.

If our hearts are set on glorifying God, then the issue will be the enjoyment of him for ever. But if our heart is set on apostasy, then the issue will be everlasting hell.

By the 'heart', Scripture means all the faculties of our souls.

We must keep a careful watch over our hearts because 'the heart is deceitful above all things and desperately wicked' (*Jer. 17:9*). 'He who trusts in his own heart is a fool' (*Prov. 28:26*).

Remember the apostle Peter. He trusted his own heart and ended up denying Christ. Are we any better than he?

We must keep a careful watch over our hearts so that they trust only in Christ for help and comfort.

Peter was kept from total apostasy by Christ's prayer: 'I

[157]

have prayed for you that your faith should not fail' (*Luke 22:32*).

We have a high priest who sympathizes with our weaknesses, because he was in all points tempted as we are, yet without sin. So let us therefore come boldly to the throne of grace, that we may obtain mercy and find grace to help in time of need (*Heb. 4:15, 16*).

Let us also hold fast to Christ's promise: 'Because you have kept my command to persevere, I also will keep you from the hour of trial which shall come upon the whole world, to test those who dwell on the earth' (*Rev. 3:10*).

All who, therefore, would be kept from the power of temptations to apostasy must keep their hearts trusting alone in Christ for help and strength.

We must keep a careful watch over our heart concerning its spiritual progress in, or its backslidings from, holiness. He who is not watchful over his own heart will be exposing himself to the danger of apostasy. We must examine our hearts by the Word of God, for it alone can discern its thoughts and intentions (*Heb. 4:12, 13*).

If we would defend ourselves from all temptations to apostasy, we must beware of trusting in the outward privileges of the church

It is a special mercy to be entrusted with the privileges of the church and the ordinances of the gospel.

The worship and its ordinances under the Old Testament were glorious because they were given by God. To the Israelites were committed the oracles of God (*Rom. 3:2*). The adoption, the glory, the covenants, the giving of the law, the service of God and the promises were all entrusted to the Israelites under the Old Testament (*Rom. 9:4, 5*). But in comparison to the worship of the New Testament, the privileges of the Old Testament ministry had no glory at all (*2 Cor. 3:10*).

So those who despise gospel ordinances are utter strangers to gospel holiness. What holiness can there be when people live in open defiance to Christ's commands? The ordinances of the gospel have been given to us by Christ for our spiritual benefit and as a means of fellowship with him. Therefore nothing must detract from their glory, and nor must they in any way be despised and held in contempt by the sinful neglect of them.

He is a spiritually thriving Christian who knows how to use the ordinances of the gospel for his spiritual growth. They are the only ordinary outward means by which the Lord Christ communicates his grace to us and by which we at the same time give him our love, praise, thanks and promises of loyalty and obedience. It is therefore certain that our growth in, or backslidings from, holiness, our faithfulness in, or apostasy from, our profession are greatly influenced by the use or abuse of these privileges.

But we are not to trust them, either for salvation or as able to keep us from falling into apostasy. By trusting in the fact that they diligently observe these ordinances, many have been deceived into a false security and so have ended in apostasy.

The religion of some is no more than going to church and staying there during the celebration of that sort of worship which they like. By this, they satisfy their consciences, especially if they are admitted to the sacraments and so are outwardly assured that they are true Christians.

Some content themselves with merely hearing the Word preached, but have no intention of examining themselves in the light of that Word. So they quickly forget what they heard and are like the man looking into a mirror and soon forgetting what he saw (*James 1:23, 24*). If this were not so, it would not be possible that so many hear the Word, but so few are brought to sincere and wholehearted obedience to it.

We must beware of deceiving ourselves that we will not fall into apostasy because we have spiritual gifts.

Some trust in the gifts of others and the satisfaction and help they get from them.

Others trust in their own gifts, their light, knowledge, spiritual abilities in prayer or speaking of the things of God.

But gifts will not keep people safe from apostasy. Jesus told us this quite clearly (*Matt. 7:22, 23*). And when the seventy returned after their successful mission rejoicing that even demons were subject to them in Christ's name, Christ told them not to rejoice in their spiritual gifts, but rather to rejoice because their names were written in heaven (*Luke 10:17–20*).

Spiritual gifts are for the confirmation of the gospel and the spiritual edification of the church. But gifts do not bring salvation and can be given to those who know nothing of grace in their hearts. So it is incumbent on all who have received spiritual gifts not to look to them as evidences of being truly regenerated, but to spiritual graces. Some have been deceived into thinking they have grace when they only have gifts. So the presence of spiritual gifts can mislead us into thinking that all is well when great apostasy is taking place.

Gifts, without grace, have no influence on the soul and they work only at special times and on special occasions. But grace affects the whole person at all times and in all duties. Grace works holy obedience in the soul. Gifts do not. Gifts are not, and can never be, the measure of our growth in grace nor can they tell us whether we are backsliding into apostasy.

Therefore, beware of trusting that because you have spiritual gifts, you will never fall into apostasy.

We must also beware of having too high an estimation of any special way of worship so as to convince ourselves we are right and all other ways of worship are wrong. True worship is always 'in spirit and in truth' (*John 4:24*). But our way of worship may not be the only way of expressing worship 'in spirit and in truth'. We must beware of the attitude which says, 'Keep to yourself. Do not come near me, for I am holier than you!' (*Isa. 65:5*). Such an attitude shows lack of love, humility, meekness and willingness to learn from others.

So, although we ought to greatly prize and work for the true ordering of the church of Christ, its purity of worship and regular administration of its ordinances, yet we must beware of thinking that our way is the best and only way of expressing true worship.

The following are some dangers that can arise from esteeming our way of ordering worship as the right and only way

Private duties of religion can be neglected. This can arise from worldliness, a predominant lust or a sinful trusting in our way of worship as the only correct way. When all these happen at the same time, the soul is in a very dangerous condition unless awakened by God. When men are satisfied with communal religious worship, and use it as an excuse for neglecting private spiritual duties, they are on the road to apostasy.

A private lust may be indulged to satisfy the flesh. This is a great work of the 'deceitfulness of sin'. It deceives the minds of men into justifying themselves in any one sin, such as pride of worship, pride in being called 'father' in a religious sense when Christ forbade it, pride of religious reputation and pride of admission to church privileges (*Matt. 23:9*).

A loose, careless, unspiritual walk may result. If we wish to be kept safe from apostasy, we must have a high regard for the privileges of the church and for the ordinances of gospel worship. If we neglect or despise them, we cast off Christ's yoke. If we do that, it is foolish to hope in him for mercy when we defy his authority.

On the other hand, if we trust in church privileges, and as a result allow ourselves to indulge in certain sins, we are on the road to apostasy.

The middle and safe way is the way by which we will find rest and peace to our souls. This way is no other than the way of a humble, careful, conscientious use of the ordinances for the spiritual growth of our souls.

Tests to see if we are spiritually benefiting by the ordinances of the gospel

We are benefiting from the ordinances if our hearts' desires are made more holy and heavenly by them, and humbled if they are not.

The purpose of the ordinances is to promote our growth in grace. When we find faith, love, delight in God, longings after grace and holiness with an increasing hatred of sin, fruitfulness in all good works and all duties of obedience, joy in spiritual things and self-abasement stirred up in us, then our hearts need not condemn us for lack of sincerity, even though we are aware of our many weaknesses and imperfections.

And if, through the power of corruptions and temptations, through the weakness of the flesh and unbelief, we sometimes do not experience any benefit to our souls, yet we may still be assured of our sincerity if we find ourselves blaming ourselves and humbling ourselves for our unprofitableness. Lack of this grace of humility has led some to reject the ordinances of the gospel as dead and useless, whilst others have grown formal, careless and spiritually barren. When all hypocritical veils and coverings are taken away and destroyed, these things will be seen to be the fruits of pride and of the deceitfulness of sin.

We are benefiting from the ordinances when spiritual things are made real and brought near to us.

When, in the preaching of the gospel, we find Jesus Christ 'clearly portrayed as crucified'; when we find ourselves obeying 'from the heart that form of doctrine delivered to us'; when we do, as it were, feel and 'handle the word of life' and the 'things hoped for' have reality in our souls, then we are truly benefiting from the ordinances (*Gal. 3:1; Rom. 6:17; 1 John 1:1; Heb. 11:1*).

But if we content ourselves with formal attendance and are satisfied that our hearts have not been touched and warmed by these ordinances, then we have every reason to be afraid.

We benefit from the ordinances when we find ourselves more diligent and watchful in all other duties of obedience that the gospel requires. When other duties are neglected and attendance on ordinances is made the excuse for their neglect, then the way is open to apostasy.

Finally, we benefit from the ordinances when we find ourselves strengthened by them to suffer for Christ and his gospel. He who has tasted how gracious Christ is in his ordinances will not easily be persuaded to part with him.

If we would defend ourselves from all temptations to apostasy, then we must beware of national sins. This has already been dealt with. We must be led by Christ and his Word and not by popular opinion, which says, 'Everybody does it!' God's Word is clear.

'Come out from among them and be separate, says the Lord. Do not touch what is unclean and I will receive you' (*2 Cor. 6:17*). We are to live in the midst of many peoples, like dew from the Lord, like showers on the grass, that does not tarry nor wait to be told what to do and how to behave by the sons of men (*Mic. 5:7*). We must be among them but not of them and certainly not corrupted by them and by national sins.

If Christians will immerse themselves in the world so as to learn their ways and be led by their opinions, they will be carried with them into eternal perdition.

Under the Old Testament, God could not trust his people to live among other people, nor others to live among them, knowing how unable they were to withstand the temptations to conform to the ways of the ungodly. So all nations were to be driven out of Canaan (*Lev. 18:30*). The neglect of God's wisdom and the transgression of his will by mixing with other nations and learning their ways led to their ruin.

Under the gospel, God's true church is to be kept pure and holy by the Holy Spirit dwelling in them and among them. God now entrusts all that are called to the obedience of faith to live in the midst of the nations. Yet he still warns them of its dangers and requires them to watch and keep themselves unspotted from the world (*James 1:27*).

Objection. 'But if we do not conform in some things to the world's customs, we shall be despised in the world and nobody will take any notice of us.'

Answer. What I mean is that submission to the world in yielding to its predominant vices, especially those vices which affect us in the place and time in which we live. Before we were converted, we did the popular thing, so now they think it strange that we no longer walk with them, and so they speak evil of us (*1 Pet. 4:3, 4*). Do we really wish to renounce God and Christ in order to be popular with the world? (*1 John 2:15–17; James 4:4*).

What we must do is to outdo the world in honesty, kindness, gentleness, usefulness, moderation of spirit, charity, compassion and readiness to help others in their need.

If we would defend ourselves from the temptations to apostasy, we must carefully avoid those special sins of professing Christians which alienate the minds of men from the gospel

We must avoid that lack of love and refusal to unite in worship and fellowship with other true Christians who may differ with us in the outward orderings of worship.

Many professing Christians do nothing useful or show any acts of kindness to their neighbours. We must avoid this sin and make ourselves as useful as possible.

A third sin of many professing Christians is spiritual pride and a censorious, judgmental spirit. This sin we must also be careful to avoid.

It is our duty, by a watchful, holy behaviour, to 'put to silence the ignorance of foolish men' and so to prove our sincerity to God and to men that 'when they defame us as evil-doers, those who revile our good conduct in Christ may be ashamed' (*1 Pet. 3:16*). By 'patient continuance in doing good', we must overcome all the evil and malice of hell.

He whose heart is confirmed by grace will continue to do good even though people are saying evil things about him. Such a man finds his reward in present happiness and in his sense of his acceptance with Christ. He says to himself and to all, 'This yoke is easy and this burden light.'

You may not be able to prevent apostasy from spreading, but you may take care that you have not helped it to spread further.

Love to the saints in all honesty, readiness to hear unjust criticisms meekly, freedom from forcing your opinions on others who are not yet ready to receive them and judging rashly supposed failures in others, readiness to have fellow-ship with all that 'love the Lord in sincerity' is what the world, sunk in apostasy, needs to see in all Christians.

Were all Christians meek, quiet, peaceable, sober, self-controlled, humble, useful, kind, gentle, willing to listen to all, cheerful in trials and troubles, always 'rejoicing in the Lord', then the world would not take offence at them, but wonder how any could live without them, and so be won over to them, making every effort to be like them. If honesty, sincerity and uprightness were seen among Christians on every occasion, how greatly it would glorify Christ!

And lastly, if Christians only judged and condemned others by living holy lives, then the world could not take offence. The practice of holiness judges all unholy persons in their hearts. And if they are upset and begin a quarrel, they will only expose their own sin and wickedness of life.

Let us beware, then, of apostasy, 'for yet a little while, and he who is coming will come and will not tarry. Now the just shall live by faith; but if anyone draws back, my soul has no pleasure in him' (*Heb. 10:37, 38*).

SOME OTHER
BANNER OF TRUTH
TITLES

THE WORKS OF JOHN OWEN

No outline can adequately summarise the significance of the life and work of John Owen (1616–1683). Summoned to preach before Parliament on several occasions, he was still only thirty-three when he addressed them on the day following the execution of King Charles I. A chaplain and adviser to Oliver Cromwell, he fell from the Protector's favour when he opposed the move to make him king. Even after the Great Ejection in 1662, he continued to enjoy some influence with Charles II who occasionally gave him money to distribute to impoverished ejected ministers. He was one of the leading Dissenters of his time.

It is, however, as an author that Owen is best known. During his lifetime he published over sixty titles of varying lengths; a dozen more appeared posthumously. Together they compose the twenty-four volume edition of his *Works* edited so ably by W. H. Goold in the mid-nineteenth century.

Owen's theology is marked by prodigious learning, profound thought and acute analysis of the human heart. Andrew Thomson, one of his biographers, says that Owen 'makes you feel when he has reached the end of his subject, that he has also exhausted it'. Both his subject matter – the great central themes of the Christian gospel – and his treatment of it – rich and satisfying, biblical and health-giving – secure him a permanent place in the galaxy of authors whose works deserve to be available for Christians in every age.

Owen's *Works* are published by the Banner of Truth Trust and are available as a set or in individual volumes. Contents of the twenty-three volumes are detailed overleaf.

CONTENTS OF THE TWENTY-THREE VOLUMES

DIVISION 1: DOCTRINAL

DIVISION 4: EXPOSITORY

THE DEATH OF DEATH
IN THE DEATH OF CHRIST

John Owen
with an introduction by J. I. Packer

'*The Death of Death in the Death of Christ* is a polemical work, designed to show, among other things, that the doctrine of universal redemption is unscriptural and destructive of the gospel. Those who see no need for doctrinal exactness and have no time for theological debates which show up divisions between Evangelicals may well regret its reappearance. Some may find the very sound of Owen's thesis so shocking that they will refuse to read his book at all. But there are signs today of a new upsurge of interest in the theology of the Bible: a new readiness to test tradition, to search the Scriptures and to think through the faith. It is to those who share this readiness that Owen's treatise is offered, in the belief that it will help us in one of the most urgent tasks facing Evangelical Christendom today – the recovery of the gospel.

'It is safe to say that no comparable exposition of the work of redemption as planned and executed by the Triune Jehovah has ever been done since Owen published his. None has been needed.'

From the Introduction

The Death of Death appears in Volume 10 of the *Works of John Owen.*

ISBN 0 85151 382 4
316pp., large paperback.